SINGING

Also by Dan Wooding:

Singing
in the
Dark

BARRY TAYLOR

with **Dan Wooding**

KINGSWAY PUBLICATIONS
EASTBOURNE

Front cover photo: Clive Manning

British Library Cataloguing in Publication Data

Taylor, Barry
 Singing in the dark: a rock n'roll roadie steps
 into the light.
 1. Christianity. Conversion of non-Christians
 I. Title II. Wooding, Dan *1940—*
 248.246092

 ISBN 0-86065-749-3

Printed in Great Britain for
KINGSWAY PUBLICATIONS LTD
1 St Anne's Road, Eastbourne, E Sussex BN21 3UN by
Richard Clay Ltd, Bungay, Suffolk.
Typeset by Nuprint Ltd, Harpenden, Herts.

Contents

Acknowledgements

I would like to express my love and gratitude to my wife, Cathy, for her unfailing support, encouragement and counsel.

Also, to Dan Wooding for his gifts, encouragement and writing skills, who gave this book shape.

To the congregation at Lake Arrowhead Christian Fellowship who have modelled for me the reality of true Christian love.

Foreword
by
Rick Wakeman

Courage is needed by us all at one time or another, but normally for just a small space of time. Thus, if our 'instant courage' has carried us through whatever crisis befell us, we heave a sigh of relief. Our courage is then locked away somewhere for the next time.

What happens, though, if for some completely inexplicable reason you're called upon for a very special kind of courage? Courage that will have to last you a lifetime? What happens if the world you're part of no longer has any meaning for you? What happens if your best friend becomes 'very religious' and you're a roadie with a heavy metal band and living a lifestyle that has as much in common with Christianity as communism has with Margaret Thatcher?

This is not just a straightforward matter of 'What happens when God enters your life?' It is more a case of 'What happens when God *wants* to enter your life?' Sadly so many are unaware that the Lord wants to be part of everybody's life, and sadly many more are unaware that he is already within them working in his own mysterious way.

One most remarkable case in point is that of Barry Taylor. There is no doubt that God was working very hard on Barry well before he was even aware of the situation, and this was a key factor in what was to happen later in his life.

With a new-found purpose and realism in life, Barry was reborn in more than one sense of the word, and not to put it too mildly, became a crusading disciple in the modern world. With strength from his new-found faith he developed a courage that was to take him to the Iron Curtain and beyond in his mission to help Christians and non-Christians who needed God.

Far-fetched? Not at all. While being no literary genius, I do feel qualified to write this foreword, as I am still a part of the rock industry that Barry became engulfed in (although I would like to point out that the outfit I am part of is unlike many such bands in the industry and if it were otherwise I too, like Barry, would no longer be part of it). I also am a Christian, although the Lord is still working very hard within me to help me achieve his purpose.

Honest, inspirational, and full of courage, Barry's story is a compulsive read. There is much to read between the lines and whether we are Christians or not, we will need to ask ourselves what we're going to do about our own levels of courage.

RICK WAKEMAN

Chapter One

'ARE WE FORGOTTEN?'

The poker-faced official, tightly gripping a walkie-talkie in his hand, motioned me away from the customs desk at Moscow International Airport.

'Come with me please,' he rasped in a strong Russian accent.

The date was June 26, 1986, and I thought I was about to leave the country that had such a deep impact on my life. My travelling companion, Ed, a Canadian Russian, had checked in separately and then officials had apparently decided to leave him alone and target me.

A sick feeling rose in my stomach as a soldier fell in line, his rifle slung over his shoulder, and I dutifully followed behind.

'What's the problem?' I whispered hoarsely to the sullen official. There was no reply. He just kept striding through the partly-empty terminal, his footsteps a hollow echo on the floor.

That very morning I had prayed, 'Lord, please orchestrate my departure.'

Now it seemed that was not going quite as I had envisaged, and I had a peculiar sense of forboding. I was taken into a tiny stuffy office, which appeared to be a rest area for the guards. I felt claustrophobic.

We all stood awkwardly there and so I repeated my question, 'Is there a problem?' My voice was calm, but was pitched higher, slightly higher than normal, I thought.

As I was concluding, another uniformed officer ambled through the door and said, in a reproving voice, 'Yes, there *is* a problem.' With that, he dragged deeply on a cigarette, and I imagined the acrid tobacco burning deep into his lungs.

He didn't, however, explain what it was. Although I tried to appear as innocent as possible, I watched in dread silence, well aware my travels during the previous two weeks could have caused my present difficulties.

My real purpose for being in the Soviet Union was not one that they would have been too happy about. I had gone there to make contact with Soviet Christians.

To prepare for the experience, I had taken an intensive course in Russian and read everything I could lay my hands on about this vast land of eleven time zones which includes fifteen Republics. I had heard that out of the 286 million people who lived in the Union of Soviet Socialist Republics, there were some 70 million or so Christians endeavouring to live for Jesus in such hostile surroundings.

More interesting to me than Red Square and the Kremlin were the lives of these believers who lived under a regime that spent much time and effort in fighting something they didn't believe in—God! As a Christian in the West I felt a responsibility to make contact with them and let them know that people *did* care about them.

I was hardly the James Bond type, and I wasn't sure I could make an impact on any one of them, but I was convinced I should at least make an effort. I also pictured these believers as broken, frightened people, living out their faith without drawing any attention to themselves.

This fallacy was soon dispelled when I encountered them. How could I ever forget the group of young people in Minsk, a large city located in Byelorussia (also known as White Russia).

I had been given the address of an official evangelical church in this city. But to find it had been a nightmare. There were no maps available, and Ed and I weren't sure if the source of the information was good, so we tried to be as secretive as we could.

I stopped older people in the street and, in hesitant Russian, asked if they knew of this particular address. We were sent in every conceivable direction, until finally we stumbled upon the church.

It was now 7.00 pm and, as we walked through the door into the sanctuary, I was thrilled to hear the choir rendering a hymn in that incredible Russian style of magnificent harmonies.

I noticed on the wall behind the choir an inscription which I interpreted to read, 'God is our strength'.

My eyes were drawn towards the young, slim man whose face was so obviously full of passion for God as he sang in the choir. After the service, he immediately made his way over to us, introduced himself as Sasha, and gave both of us a bear hug. Then, after giving me a brief, appraising eye, he whispered, 'Come to my house.'

Not knowing what to expect, Ed and I looked at each other and smiled. 'Why not?' we said in unison.

We took a bus from the church. As the three of us stood in the aisle of a noisy vehicle, none of us said very much, but just kept smiling at each other.

Sasha's 'home' was one cramped room in an old house which was divided up and shared with about six other families. There was a communal kitchen, and an old outhouse was shared with the other residents. I caught the smell of a sewer flowing nearby and the crumbling building reeked of mustiness.

This was my first visit to a Russian home. I gazed around the tiny room. With its sparse furnishings, it gave the impression of being airless. Sasha motioned us to the only sitting place in the room—a mattress on the floor that doubled as both bed and couch. They had a sideboard with a bunch of pictures of those presumed to be family members. The peeling greyish well was bare.

Sasha introduced us in Russian to Anna, his wife, and Nicholai, their young son.

He pointed to a Japanese 'ghetto-blaster' that he said he had bought on the black market. 'Besides my Bible, this is my most prized possession,' he smiled.

Sasha explained that he and his wife were musicians. During the summertime they would travel with a friend around the country and sing Christian songs at secret youth camps.

'I write my songs and then sing them into this cassette player,' he explained.

'Would you like to hear some of them?' he asked.

We nodded with enthusiasm.

I was astonished to hear his contemporary songs which were so different from the older hymns we had just heard at the church. Although they were sombre, they reflected his deep love for God.

I asked Sasha what his needs were. 'We always need Bibles, but I could sure use a drum machine,' he said. He was well versed in Western musical technology and he knew what was good and what wasn't.

'I would use it to make my music better and gain the interest of more young people,' he explained. 'If your music here sounds like Western music, you have more opportunity to share the message of the gospel.'

We talked a lot about music. I shared the story of where I had come from and my deep involvement with rock music in the West.

Sasha sat on the floor, his shoulder leaning against the sideboard. Suddenly he became very serious.

'My great burden is for young people in this country,' he said, his voice rising. 'The system doesn't offer them much hope. They are filled with Marxist ideology and sold a lot of lies. Most of them don't buy it— but they don't know what else there is.'

I said nothing but indicated that I wanted to hear more.

'What they really need is a relationship with God, but they have been told that God doesn't exist and, like most young people, they look at the church and see lots of old people who they are told are fools. It's common for Russian schoolchildren to be taken to old church buildings that have been converted into atheist museums where they are shown the "myths and fables" of Christianity, and these are unfavourable compared with the advances of "scientific socialism". In many small or large Soviet towns you can find small museums carrying blurred pictures of so-called events that visitors are told are "child sacrifices" and Christians "drinking blood".

'But our young people have an incredible fascination with the West, especially its clothes and music. Any information we can bring from you about the West is used like a status symbol. They can hear some Western music on the radio and often music tapes circulate underground.

'So Anna, myself, and a friend travel around as much as we can, singing and sharing the real hope that we've found in God.'

I thought, as I listened to Sasha, that the last thing Soviet youth needed was our so-called Western culture. Obviously it provided temporary relief from their grey existence but, as I had personally experienced, it didn't answer any of the real problems in life. For me, it was pure escapism. Still, I was glad to see one young believer utilise that desire for things Western as a means to bring real hope to people.

As Sasha walked Ed and me to the nearest bus stop, he said, 'Meet me at the town square tomorrow evening at six o'clock. I want you to meet some friends of mine.'

Intrigued, Ed and I turned up in the centre of town the next day and found Sasha already waiting. Without acknowledging us, he immediately began to walk towards a nearby bus stop, and we fell into line behind him.

After boarding an old, wheezing bus, I allowed my eyes to move from side to side as the vehicle racketed through the bleak uniformity of the suburban sprawl. I watched rows of dreary grey tenement buildings pass by. They looked as if they hadn't been painted for years. A tangle of television aerials sprang from them, reaching up to the 'eye' that brought down its images from the sky.

After a twenty-minute ride, the bus disgorged us on

the outskirts of the city and Sasha led us through this alien territory to an old building. We followed him down into the basement.

Not quite sure of what to expect, I was surprised to see the room full of young people. They were sitting on old rickety benches in an attitude of prayer.

'Welcome to our Bible school,' said Sasha, cutting across the sounds of the praying young people. 'I come here most nights with some friends, and we gather with the young people here to pray for our nation, that God would use us to reach it with his message of love and salvation.'

It was an unforgettable night. The group ranged in age from twelve to eighteen. As we talked, I discovered that some were from Christian families, while others had parents who were active in the Communist Party. Each one was totally committed to seeing their nation changed. It was a great risk for them to be there, as it was obviously an illegal meeting. But these committed young Soviet believers weren't deterred by the fear of arrest or imprisonment.

They were well aware of the danger they were in, but appeared quite prepared to pay the price, whatever it might be. Some confided that they were certain their future would hold some persecution.

I only had one Russian Bible with me, and I felt prompted by God to hand it to a young man who told me his father was in prison for pastoring an illegal church.

'I have settled in my heart that, whatever the cost, I will follow in my father's footsteps,' he declared, his eyes shining with conviction.

I was moved as I listened. I had heard stories of pastors—men and women—who had gone through much hardship for the gospel's sake, but these were teenagers. In the West, and in my own case, my teenage years had been spent in rebellion, anger and general foolishness. But here was a group of young people who had made a choice of how they were going to live, no matter what the cost. Their heart for God challenged me and caused me to examine my priorities. Here they were living in a country full of struggle and deprivation, with so little of what I had taken for granted, yet making choices that were sure to add to their difficulties. Their lives were focused not on material benefit, but on Jesus Christ.

As the trip progressed, I discovered they were not the only group of people who displayed that same courage and conviction.

As I stood in that sparse room at Moscow Airport, I did not know what the officials were looking for. Maybe I'd been followed, or it may have just been a random check. I had nothing tangible with me to incriminate myself or anyone else. But I did have something they could never find—a message in my heart.

It was a promise I had made not only to Sasha and his friends, but to many of the believers I had encountered on my travels. It was a promise I had made in response to a question, one I was asked many times.

'Are we forgotten?' they asked of me in gently reproving tones.

I told these believers that I would do everything within my power to make sure they were *never* forgotten. The umbilical cord between believers in the West and those in the Soviet Union had been severed by the Iron Curtain; now I wanted to see that cord restored again.

By now I was standing in my underwear as the

guards gave my belongings their keen unblinking scrutiny.

'Have you found anything?' I understood one of them to ask.

'*Nyet!*' came the reply, obviously disappointed.

'Okay,' he said turning to me, but never allowing his dark eyes to meet mine, 'you can leave.' He swiftly changed his expression like a chameleon.

Wrenching my mind back to the present, and somewhat relieved, I hastily pulled on my clothing and headed out of the room to the plane.

As the Aeroflot jet zoomed down the runway and climbed en route for Helsinki in Finland, I looked out of the window. Moscow soon disappeared from view as we rose into the cotton-wool clouds. But the faces of those believers were still vivid in my mind.

Their question kept haunting me: 'Are we forgotten?' I hoped the answer would be no, but what could I really do about it? After all I was just a solitary Englishman. But at least I knew what my mission in life was to be.

Chapter Two

POPPING PILLS

I cracked a couple of eggs and dropped them into the frying pan in my home in Huntingdon, a pleasant market town eighteen miles north-west of the university city of Cambridge. I was aware of my mother hovering in the kitchen as my glazed eyes vainly tried to focus on the eggs.

'What are you doing, luv?' she asked gently.

'What do you think I'm doing? I'm frying some eggs,' I snapped. It seemed obvious to me.

'Well don't you think you should turn the gas on first?' she responded in an even voice.

I wasn't sure how to reply. Of course I should have, but when you're trying to fry eggs after taking LSD, it's easy to overlook the obvious.

My mother looked at me strangely and asked, 'Are you all right, son?'

'Yes, mum. I just forgot,' I responded with a wide, foolish, drugged-out grin.

My mother didn't realise what I had been up to. After all, she wanted to think the best of her elder son, and I was only fifteen. She had probably never even heard of LSD; in fact she hardly knew who the Beatles were.

There was nothing traumatic happening in my home. We were an ordinary working-class family. My father, Dennis, was employed by a gas pipe installation company, my mum sold confectionary in a sweet shop and I had a younger brother, Brian. Our home was owned by the local council and our lives were predictable within the class structure of our environment. There were no tantrums in our house—just a group of loosely connected people who were not big on communication. We were an intense and rather silent family. The house and its furniture provided props for a charade that my life had become.

Maybe going to Hinchingbrooke, a historic grammar school, had widened my horizons, but something in me, instead of making the most of the opportunity to advance, chose to self-destruct instead. There was no way I would follow in the footsteps of Oliver Cromwell and diarist Samuel Pepys, who both went to the local Huntingdon Free School. The incredible history of the hallowed corridors never once impacted me, even though I discovered that this building was initially a Benedictine nunnery founded by William the Conqueror around 1087.

Something was going on inside Barry Taylor's head, but I certainly wasn't aware what it was. I certainly wasn't finding any answers or challenge at school. Latin just wasn't providing the excitement I craved. I found school a stultifying exercise that did nothing more than button up my already introspective personality. One word summed up my assessment of school—*boring*.

Around the corner from our house lived the

O'Reillies, a tough Irish family. John, one of their children, was following in the footsteps of his elder brothers, embarking on a life of hooliganism. A 'skinhead', John was a pretty good shoplifter and always ready for a fight—which he usually started. He scared the living daylights out of me, and yet his violent persona held a deep fascination for me.

For some strange reason, John liked me too. I never fathomed that, as I was the total opposite, though it could have been that both our mothers went to bingo together every Friday night! Although he intimidated me and I didn't know how to relate to him, I liked the idea of knowing someone who was older and who, in a strange way, seemed to have a handle on where he was going in life.

At my age, even a life of crime seemed to be preferable to a boring existence in a terraced house on Coronation Avenue.

John who was an old seventeen, spent every Friday night in a pub called The Lord Protector—named after Oliver Cromwell. The place had a Friday night disco which, as far as I was concerned, was the only exciting thing that ever happened in our town.

However, I had a serious problem. I possessed a baby face which ensured I could never gain admittance to the disco.

'You're too young,' the bouncers would growl each time I attempted to penetrate this world of strobe lighting and loud, throbbing music. 'Clear off, kid, before we have to change your nappy for you!'

My fortune changed, however, when I began hanging out with John O'Reilly. With a menacing promise of violence, O'Reilly would scowl at the bouncers and say, 'This kid's with me. Let him in.'

With this new development, life began to take on a

new meaning in more ways than one. John and his friends were heavily involved in drugs, which were readily available in Huntingdon. O'Reilly never forced me to take any, but I was intrigued with the way they appeared to bring him even more alive.

One fateful Friday night, as the ceiling vibrated to the sound of the Supremes singing 'Baby Love', I shouted in John's ear, 'What's it like to take that stuff?'

A Cheshire Cat grin that enveloped his wide Irish face indicated that it was great.

'Why don't you try some speed, Barry? It will make you feel good,' he said producing a bag of peanuts. When he saw a confused look sweeping my face, he hissed, 'The pills are hidden between them. That way you can eat them in public and no one will know what you are doing.'

I'd never really done anything illicit in my life up to that point. But I decided to give 'speed' a try.

Reaching into the bag, I took a handful of peanuts and a few pills and washed them down with a swig of Coca-Cola. I didn't particularly relish the taste, which to my palate seemed like strong aspirin tablets. At first, I thought I was going to throw them straight back up, but not wanting to appear stupid, I forced myself to hang onto them. I soon forgot the unsettling feeling in my stomach as the drugs began to affect my brain. A strange sensation took over my body, like pins and needles all over.

My heart began to pound incredibly fast and I became very animated. I started to talk with everyone without my usual inhibitions. I was normally shy, but now I had no qualms to rap with anyone about anything. My emotions were usually locked deeply away from everyone around me, but speed unlocked them and brought them out.

The Lord Protector became my place of liberation, or so I thought. The high decibel black soul music that blared and thumped from the disco floor became the background for my weekly excursions into the land of chemical fantasy.

I would stagger home in the early hours of Saturday morning, long after my parents had gone to bed, and spend the rest of the night indulging in drug-induced fantasies, waiting for the effects of the drugs to wear off. I'd sit on my bed for hours in total silence as my brain raced with strange thoughts.

I didn't really like how I felt the morning after. I'd be tired, depressed, and my mouth would feel as if someone had parked a car in it. Still, that was a price I was prepared to pay for a few hours without inhibition.

John and his friends introduced me to many different kinds of drugs after that, all of which I thoroughly enjoyed. After a few years my body began to suffer from the effects, but when you're young, you do have a sense of your own immortality.

'Nothing bad will ever happen to me,' was my proud boast to myself. 'I can handle it.'

I was still haunted by questions that drove me nuts. I analysed everything, trying to find reasons for the lives we led—and mine in particular. While I never had any cosmic revelations with any of these drugs, at the time they certainly seemed a lot more exciting and fulfilling than hour after hour of maths, physics and biology at school. Needless to say, my Friday night experiences eventually became an almost daily experience.

I took a paper round so I could buy more drugs

from the various pushers around town. I was pretty successful at keeping it together and not having people know that I was even on drugs. Even my school friends had no idea what I was up to. Strangely enough, even though I was committed to this drug lifestyle, it wasn't something that I felt I could actively promote to anyone else. Something inside told me that it was ultimately destructive.

At grammar school, the faculty laboured on academics. It was meant to prepare people for university and a great future in education. But to me it was all a waste of time. I retreated more and more into my drug world and just scoffed at education.

Like the LSD guru, Dr Timothy Leary, once said, 'Turn On, Tune In, Drop Out.' That's all I wanted to do.

The only thing I did know was that I wanted out of the town I lived in. In fact I wanted out of England, wishing to explore new frontiers. Throughout all of this time, there were only four things that fascinated me: music, drugs, languages and geography. I was particularly interested in how people lived in other places and I had a real desire to get out and see the world.

When I was seventeen, I spent the bulk of my time on drugs with a friend named Kevin who lived around the corner. We met on our paper rounds. Kevin was a reckless but friendly chap. He was a borderline hooligan, not in the same league as John O'Reilly.

By now other discos had started up, and we would go to different ones around the area, 'pop pills' and dance the night away, often oblivious to our ridiculous, maniacal behaviour.

One Thursday morning I dragged myself out of bed to do my paper round and walked bleary-eyed into the local newsagent's shop where I worked. I took my papers and set off on my bike on my usual round. When I was finished, I returned to the shop to drop off my bag and when I walked in, Scotty, the manager, said, 'Did you hear about Kevin?'

I shook my head blankly.

'He was killed last night in a car crash,' he said in a matter-of-fact way. 'The chap he was with was drunk and wrapped the car around a lamp post. Kevin was killed instantly.' Scotty seemed to be unreasonably detached from the horror he had just imparted to me.

But the news was like a rocket fired into my heart. It was a grievous blow. I didn't know how to react to this. Kevin dead! No, he couldn't be. I had seen him the day before and we had planned our weekend together.

He was just too young to die. I felt a dragging sense of bewildered desolation. This was something I could not understand and no one could explain to me.

Now I knew I definitely wanted out. I increased my drug intake and became even more reclusive. I went through the motions of school, knowing that in a few months I would graduate. But then, instead of waiting for that to happen, I decided to walk out. The futility of my life overwhelmed me and so I decided to get a job, earn some money, and get out of England.

By this point, the channels of meaningful communication with my parents had completely dried up. When I announced I had quit school, they just stared blankly at me and said nothing. They had, by now, realised that they were not getting through to me and so any negative communication from them would be futile. My mother generally attempted to understand, but talk with my father had virtually ground to a halt.

I worked for a few months at a printing factory in

the town and saved up enough money to go onto the Continent. Mark, another friend, agreed to go with me and we decided on Holland because Mark said he knew of a potential job opportunity in Delft.

We got the job—in a fruit-packing factory—but Mark wasn't too happy and after a couple of weeks he decided to return home. I stayed in Delft for another nine months, living a monk-like existence. I rented a room from a Dutch family and spent most of my time alone.

Because I didn't speak Dutch, I spent most of my time locked in my room, reading philosophical books by writers like Hermann Hesse and Thomas Mann. It was my way of trying to work out what an eighteen-year-old on this planet was supposed to be doing with his life. I never read, however, the words of John Bunyan: 'the way is the way, and there is an end.'

I didn't find Bunyan's 'way' in Holland. People there seemed to share the same problems as those living in England. The one reality I discovered in my shifting world, however, was that being in a different geographical place doesn't alter what's going on inside you. If it's bad, it's bad, regardless of where your body is parked.

I returned to Huntingdon a little more travelled but just as confused as when I'd left. I was beginning to wonder if I wasn't just crazy and trying too hard to understand life. It was like a nagging headache that wouldn't go away.

Maybe I should forget about trying to discover the meaning of life, and concentrate on the real issue— like having fun, doing as little work as possible and ingesting all the drugs I possibly could.

Chapter Three

TARTAN TERROR

A wall of hysterical screams greeted my friend Ian and me as we pulled up in a rental truck outside the Apollo Theatre in Glasgow. As I peered through the windshield at thousands of girls dressed from head to toe in tartan, I turned to Ian, who was also from Huntingdon, and remarked, 'This is absolutely nuts.'

The sobbing pubescent fans carrying placards inscribed with 'Ian, Eric, Les; Derek and Woody— We Love You!' surged forward and pressed against the truck. They assumed that hidden away with us were the Bay City Rollers, but instead all the vehicle contained was the Scottish teeny-bop group's stage equipment.

As Ian edged the truck slowly through this hysterical throng, I continued to gawk at the scene. Police vainly tried to clear a way for us to get to the Apollo loading dock, but the girls wouldn't accept that the band was not in the van.

Eventually we made it, and as we climbed out of the cab, the girls pressed in around us and screamed,

'Where are they? We love them.'

This bizarre scene took place just six weeks after I had returned from the land of tulips and wooden shoes. I had met a couple of older guys, Pete and his friend Derek, at The Lord Protector during a Friday night session.

These two seemed different from the regulars at the pub, although they knew most of the people there. They were into Jackson Browne and the Eagles as well as satin American baseball jackets, which was quite a contrast to the general skinhead attire of two-tone iridescent trousers, shortened to a ridiculous length, held up with ultra-thin braces, button-down Oxford shirts and finished off with the classic Dr Martin air-cushioned bovver boots, which was the attire of choice among the general populace of the Lord Protector. Derek was a guitarist and Pete worked with him. They appeared a little more worldly-wise than most of my associates.

We developed a friendship. I think at first they patronised me because I was usually so 'out of my brains' on drugs. The pills unleashed my tongue and probably drove everyone else crazy. The pair soon discovered that when I was off drugs, I never spoke, but they didn't seem to care.

The first time I went to Pete's home, I sat on a settee for two hours doing a zombie impression, never uttering a word.

Derek, Pete and Angus, their dog, who seemed almost human and experienced most of the drugs and booze they did, had secured a house to rent close to my home, and I spent most of my spare time there. Eventually, without any formal arrangement, I moved in with them.

They were great guys and had some really interesting friends. Ian, Derek's brother, worked as a road manager for the keyboard 'Caped Crusader' Rick Wakeman, and he often popped in from London with an assortment of Wakeman's musicians, as well as other music business friends. Pete and Derek's house became the weekend party hangout for anyone who wanted to just drop in.

Derek had a knack of turning any living environment into a quasi-recording studio. Once he had found a good room, which was usually the living room, within hours it would be cluttered with amplifiers and guitars and drums. After a few beers, Pete would fancy himself as quite a rock singer, and so we had many fun hours of 'making music' (and keeping the neighbours awake) in this small terraced house.

Quite regularly there would be thumps on the wall from next door followed by shouts of 'Turn it down!' We usually ignored the thumps, especially if they were in time with the music.

All of these guys were so full of life and possessed a zest for living that it started to open me up inside. After my time of relative isolation in Holland, I became a little more active in the human race again.

I hadn't worked since I returned from Holland, and I wasn't sure whether I would go back there or to another country. But Pete came up with a suggestion that sounded really interesting.

'Barry, Ian just called,' he said, as I walked through the door after visiting my parents. 'He's going out on the road for six weeks with a group called The Bay City Rollers and needs someone to help with loading the equipment. Do you fancy doing it? It's great money. I can't do it because I've got another job. Why don't you give it a whirl.'

After a brief discussion on the music merits of the

Rollers, who were certainly not my favourite band at the time, even though they were being touted as the 'new Beatles', we decided that the money that could be earned in six weeks far surpassed the pain of having to endure their 'music'.

The group got their name when their mentor/manager Tom Paton arbitrarily stuck a pin in a U.S. map and hit Bay City, Michigan. Thus the Bay City Rollers were born.

The first gig was to be in Glasgow. I didn't really have a clue what I was doing, but following Ian's lead, I picked up equipment from the truck and carried it on stage and put it where he told me. It was not exactly a difficult job for the money.

Most of the other 'roadies' were Scots and were quite jaded, having been around the music business for years and had seen (and experienced) it all. But to me it was all quite fascinating.

That experience at the Apollo was total madness. The girls that were outside continued to scream all day long as well as bang on the doors of the theatre. It was impossible to get outside for the 'tartan terror' surrounding the place.

Shortly before the show was to begin, the Rollers were smuggled inside. Then it was show time, à la The Bay City Rollers. Once the band took the stage, clad in their tartan uniforms highlighted by knicker-length pants, pandemonium erupted. In fact, every night the same decibel-breaking 'Rollermania' would issue forth. The noise was deafening. I'd never seen so many teenage girls hysterically crying in one place before. The Rollers provoked a genuine outbreak of teenage frenzy reminiscent of Beatlemania in the early sixties.

We all wondered why we bothered to set up any

equipment because the general sequence of events was that as soon as the band started to play, their 'music' was drowned out by the screams of the kids who then attempted any way that they could to storm the stage and get a piece of their favourite Roller.

All of the crew, including myself, spent every night pulling fainting girls out of the orchestra pit, dragging away those who had successfully made it to the hallowed ground of the stage. It was an unusual way to make a living and certainly more lively than packing fruit in Holland.

Half way through the tour, one of the guys in charge of the sound equipment was suddenly called away due to a personal problem. There was no time to bring in another sound engineer, so he gave me a quick lesson in how to work the board.

'Just stick to the basics, Barry, and you'll do fine,' he told me.

I discovered I had a knack for it. Before long I had ceased unloading the truck each night and engaging in hand-to-hand combat with the teenagers. Now I was mixing the sound for the band on stage.

After the tour finished, the sound company responsible for the tour offered me a staff job. I was delighted to accept. It seemed to me to be a great way to earn a living.

I soon forgot all of my frustrations with life, temporarily at least. I began to travel all over Europe with different bands and singers, including Marvin Gaye, Daryl Hall and John Oates, Gladys Knight and the Pips. I even did glam-rock Gary Glitter's 'First Farewell Tour'. The latter was as much a scream as the Bay City Rollers' tour because of the similar fanatical response of the girl fans.

We were at the Batley Variety Club in Yorkshire,

in the middle of one particularly gruelling tour of night clubs in England, with the Stylistics, a soul group from America. Ian got a call from a friend of his who was working for 'a band from Australia' that was looking for a permanent road crew.

As much as the money they offered, the big appeal was the fact that they were going to America, land of 'The Rockford Files' and Elvis. With the thought of three more weeks of British clubs that smelt of old beer, rotten food and stale smoke, there was no competition: Ian and I both decided to go for it.

They were called AC-DC and had been formed in Sydney in 1973. I'd never actually heard of them before, but the guy who called us for the job told us they were 'great'. Of course, we'd been with our share of not-so-great bands, and we were in the business probably more for the money and the lifestyle than the music.

We first met the band in Dover at the Sea-Link ferry terminal. The group had just arrived from Australia and were about to embark on a European tour supporting the British heavy metal band, Black Sabbath, whose lead singer was still Ozzy Osbourne. They then comprised Bon Scott the singer, Angus and Malcolm Young two brothers who played guitar, Phil Rudd the drummer, and Mark Evans the bass player. After all of the slick, shiny-suited soul groups and teeny bopper bands and occasional American country and western singers, these guys looked almost human. None of them were very tall and their idea of getting dressed up was jeans and a tee-shirt. They were friendly and didn't appear to be plagued with that rock and roll 'posers' attitude that we so often encountered from others. There was an immediate rapport between us as we began to exchange in rapid fashion lots of 'g'days'.

I still hadn't heard any of their music—even after the first gig, I still hadn't really heard it. On that first night in Paris, Ian and I saw their equipment and groaned. To say the least, it was knocked around. They had a lot of loud speakers that had to be wired in a specific way. And because they were the support group, there wasn't much time for them to do a sound check or practice.

Ian and I set up their equipment and waited with eager anticipation for them to take the stage. They didn't stay very long. Their equipment functioned even worse than it looked. Most of the cables were faulty and their amplifiers had the wrong fuses and blew up. The drum kit kept sliding across the floor and the sound was terrible.

They made it through a few songs and decided to call it quits and leave the stage to make way for Ozzy and his wild men.

Ian and I both figured we were going to be back in England quicker than we thought. We walked into the AC-DC dressing room expecting to be read the riot act, but amazingly the band apologised to us for the appalling state of their equipment.

The next day we managed to repair most of it and get it functioning. Once we could hear them, we discovered they really were a great band, playing a gutsy brand of rock music. They have since been branded as a satanic band, and I've heard all sorts of stories of what their name means and the things they are alleged to get up to, but in all my time with them, the closest they came to satanic worship was watching 'The Adams Family' on television.

And as far as I could tell, their name was more related to electricity than anything else.

The tour through Europe went well and America beckoned. I certainly didn't regret the path that I had chosen, but I wasn't quite sure where it was all leading and what difference it would make.

Chapter Four

THE SCREAMING SKULL

I gazed in disbelief at the enormous pile of food on my plate. 'I thought I was getting a sandwich, but this is a Sunday dinner between two slices of bread,' I shouted to Ian as we sat in the Carnegie Deli on New York's Broadway. 'It's absolutely amazing. You'd need a snake's hinged jaw to eat this.'

This was my introduction to America. My first lesson in the 'land of the brave and free' was that even ordering a sandwich can be a complicated process. Unlike the classic British Rail 'cheese and tomato special', the American choice is endless.

'What kind of bread do you want, honey? There's wheat, rye, pumpernickel, sourdough,' the waitress asked. 'Do you want lettuce, tomato, mustard, mayonnaise, pickles?'

My head was spinning with the choices she gave me. I settled for a roast beef sandwich on white bread 'as simple as possible'.

Ian had picked me up at JFK Airport and brought me direct to the deli located in New York's theatre district. Ian loved American food, in fact he loved America. Hurrying past that New York window paraded the wildest cross section of humanity I'd ever seen in one place. All seemed to be in an incredible rush to get somewhere—business people, wild aliens from other planets with hair-styles that looked like they had been caused by electric volts being passed through their heads. They all seemed to be drawn to the 'Big Apple' like maggots to a mouldy piece of fruit. In that steamy hot cauldron there was even an old tramp walking down the street playing a pair of drumsticks on the pavement.

Ian told me that I had one day to recover from 'jet lag' and then we had a 'little drive to Texas'. We picked up a rental truck, drove to the cargo terminal at JFK and loaded up the band's gear. We had three days to get to our first venue in Austin, Texas.

I'd seen some wild crowds in my time, but nothing compared to the Texas audience. The first show was to take place at The Armadillo World Headquarters, which apparently was some kind of a vague reference to stoned armadillos. It was a huge indoor barnlike building which seated 5,000 very boisterous Texans in varying states of narcotic and alcoholic decay.

They really liked AC-DC. The first concert was a roaring success. We set out on the rest of our tour suitably excited about the possibility of the band really making it big in America. That first AC-DC tour was mostly in support of established American rock bands and performers like Aerosmith, Ted Nugent, Foreigner and Kiss. The band, and Ian and myself, got a taste of the huge arena concerts that America is famous for.

A band of Aussies and a couple of Brits were a novelty throughout America. The simple fact was that our foreign accents were a drawing card. It was amazing that saying 'hello luv' could open so many doors. We also discovered that in America the rock-and-roll lifestyle of girls, booze, drugs and parties was a magnified version of that in Europe—and of course we stepped right in.

Although it was hard work—we generally had to drive three or four hundred miles after every concert to get to the next one—it was also great fun. But towards the end of our first tour we found ourselves taking drugs like speed more to stay awake and get our job done than for pleasure.

In that first tour we covered some 40,000 miles, zigzagging the country. One day it was Chicago, a couple of days later Miami. There were times when we could have killed the booking agent, but we certainly got a taste of the diversity of the American lifestyle. And we could tell anyone we met the best truck stops to go to on any freeway in the country, as we fast became truck-stop connoisseurs.

The United States was an important market for the band and, over the next couple of years, AC-DC spent an increasing amount of time playing concerts there. Each time they returned, the reception was getting so much more positive, the venues larger, until finally AC-DC was the main attraction and had reached the stage where Ian and I had been joined by three articulated lorries, two luxury buses to travel on, and about twenty-five other guys. We became a strange but fun-filled family of foreigners wreaking havoc wherever we went. We were an odd bunch, most of the guys being from Birmingham, with a few East Anglians like Ian and myself thrown in for good measure.

One of my non-paying jobs was to translate Brummie vernacular into understandable English for the

many frustrated and confused waitresses, hotel recep-
tionists and promoters that we met along our way.

Our buses became 'parties on wheels', with plenty
of booze raided from dressing rooms as well as drugs
and a constant supply of American girls. In fact we on
the road crew tended to fare better than the band,
because they weren't around so much, so we tended to
syphon the best 'talent' onto our bus.

From America we travelled the world with this big
family, and pretty soon one country blended into the
next, venue into venue. It really didn't matter where
we were, there was work to be done as quickly as
possible, drugs to procure, girls to chat up and, every
once in a while, sleep to be taken.

I spent less and less time in Huntingdon and more
and more time on the road. When AC/DC was off the
road, I would do other little tours just to consume my
time. This was at the inception of the punk movement,
and so we long-hairs would go and do sound for bands
like X-Ray Specs and Souixie and the Banshees,
which was an experience in itself. I would watch
fascinated from the side of the stage as the punkers
would 'slam dance', butt one another in the head and
spit in every direction. It made me feel quite staid and
AC-DC quite pedestrian.

Whenever I came back home, I looked upon it as a
holiday. By this time, Derek had left England and
moved to Los Angeles with another friend with the
hope of making it in the music business there. Our
paths had never really crossed in all the times that I'd
been in the States, but we kept in touch through
letters and phone calls.

I'd been on the road for about ten months and
arrived home just before Christmas. When I arrived

at our house, Pete greeted me by saying, 'We've had a weird letter from Derek.'

He handed me what looked more like a book. There was page after page of Derek's handwriting. In it, Derek talked about becoming a Christian, which neither Pete nor I could really understand since we were English and generally nice guys. And we took Religious Education at school.

We scanned through his letter, but got bored with all the Bible references and so we chalked it up to the simple fact that he was living in L.A. and that really explained everything. We regarded this new situation with a sceptical eye. Everyone knew L.A. was the final resting place of most of the weirdness on this planet. All the fruits and nuts were reported to have gravitated there.

Something bugged me, however, And this was because I knew Derek. We'd done all kinds of drugs together and he wasn't the type of person who would run off and get involved in a strange religious cult. There were other things that bothered me as well. Although the past three or four years had been exciting and I'd seen a lot, some old questions began to haunt me again—especially about the meaning of my life here on Spaceship Earth.

I reflected on this lifestyle. Rock and roll was all very well, and travelling the world was a great opportunity, but certain questions were still there. What is the point of all this? What am I really supposed to do with my life?

Terry, who was the lighting guy for the band, had a pet nickname for me. Once in a while he affectionately called me 'The Screaming Skull'. The reason was I seldom allowed my pale English skin to see the light of day and I had developed a penchant for wearing black and, with my long hair, Terry seemed to think that I looked a bit like a walking skeleton. It didn't bother me, but one day, after a particularly hard night of drugs, I went into the hotel bathroom and looked at myself in the mirror. For some reason his nickname lodged in my mind. For the first time in years, I took stock of the man in the mirror, and I wasn't too pleased with what I saw.

It wasn't just the appearance of a body that had taken too many drugs. All of a sudden, it was as though I was confronted with the reality of what was in my heart. Emptiness.

Because I still didn't have any answers, I just carried on, but with a renewed sense of searching. I knew that I couldn't go on for ever like this, and once again that old 'you're just crazy' feeling filled my head. No one else seemed to be too bothered about anything. Or, if they were, they weren't saying much about it.

There was something else about Derek's letter that bothered me. Why Christianity? It seemed the least appealing of any of the ideologies floating around the world. In fact, Derek's turning to Christianity was all the stranger to me because the only person that I really knew who claimed something special about their Christianity was my grandmother. And I couldn't see what my grandmother and Derek could possibly share in common. But I left it at that and Pete and I joked about it a bit and told ourselves that he'd snap out of it. He didn't.

Derek finally did make it in music, but it was in the Christian music arena. With some friends, he recorded an album of songs about his relationship with God and this was sent to us along with a constant supply of 'Epistles according to Derek'. This became the source of many conversations among our group of friends in Huntingdon. We justified the fact that we obviously already were Christians but, unlike Derek, we didn't need to preach about it. We just *were* and that was it.

We brooded on the problem, and eventually hit upon an admirable solution. We would do the good Christian thing and go to the Christmas Eve service at the local church around the corner from the pub. Once 'last orders' had been called at the Black Bull, another local hangout, a small group of us made our way to the midnight service at this ancient church and heartily joined in the carol singing, having been primed by the annual visit from the Salvation Army who had sung with gusto.

In some ways it threw a bit of a wet blanket over our usual Christmas festivities because the conversation kept coming around to this 'Christian thing' and none of us really knew what to do about it. Still, we felt like good Boy Scouts who had done their duty.

Our other friends all had their varying opinions which ranged from 'I always knew Derek wasn't quite all there,' to, 'If that's what he wants to do with his life, that's fine for him. But he shouldn't start preaching at me.'

We began another arduous slog around the globe. In some ways I was quite glad to get back on the road. But somehow the magic wasn't there any more, at least for me. I found myself once more becoming self-absorbed and analytical. I wanted to throw myself into my usual round of drugs, and escapism, but I couldn't do it with the same vigour that I had done before. I'd also begun to notice that a few people I had met in the course of my travels weren't around any more. A couple of them had died, others had got burned out. I discovered that the source of their demise was drug-related, and I started to wonder if maybe that old stand-by, 'It'll never happen to me,' wasn't becoming a riskier statement to make.

I also didn't have a clue how I was going to change all these things. Once or twice when I'd been particularly burned out from the hard work and long hours, coupled with self-abuse, I'd considered an early retirement from the music business, but then I was confronted with, well, what am I going to do then? I'm going to go back to Huntingdon? And do what?

What could really top this life that I was living? I was earning great money, travelling, eating in expensive restaurants, meeting rock-and-roll stars and going to a concert almost every night. Not too bad of a life, really.

Was it?

Chapter Five

THE MAN IN BLACK

I was dressed in my usual attire—a black motorcycle jacket, black tee-shirt and jeans, and three dangling earrings, not black, but silver, attached to two rather pink ears.

While the lighting and sound equipment was being unloaded in Phoenix, Arizona, by the union crew, I decided to use the spare time to go on a mission; to locate a bookstore where I could buy a Bible. This was definitely not an everyday occurrence for me, but something I felt I had to do for the sake of Derek, my poor deluded friend.

I found a Christian bookstore close by. To my surprise, as I walked through the door I felt scared. However, I was sure that I was not as apprehensive as the lady behind the counter. I'm sure she had not had too many 'screaming skulls' walking into the shop before.

'Do you have a Bible I could buy, luv?' I asked her as she cowered behind the counter.

There was a long pause as she gazed at me, her

mouth agape. Perhaps she thought that I was casing the joint to rob it. Little did she know that underneath this dark exterior was a wimpy Englishman.

She eventually overcame her fear and brought out a selection of Bibles for me to choose from. I left the shop carrying a large Open Study Bible under my arm. I then stopped at a nearby liquor store and bought a copy of *Rolling Stone* magazine.

The large guy behind the counter there looked strangely at me as he spotted my leather-bound Bible.

'Excuse me, sir,' I asked hesitantly, 'do you have a big bag to put these items in.'

He looked at me as if I should be locked up, but handed over a large brown bag into which I put the Bible and magazine.

When I climbed on board the tour bus, I put my Bible in a safe place by my bunk and resumed my career with the band. I reassured myself that the Bible wasn't for me, but to help my friend Derek. He was definitely in serious trouble now that he had become what is commonly known as a 'religious nut'.

We had come to Arizona by way of Los Angeles and, for the first time in a couple of years, I had the opportunity—or was it misfortune?—of spending time with Derek there. I knew I would have some time off in Los Angeles and before arriving there I had called Derek from Chicago to tell him of my imminent arrival in the 'City of the Angels'. I knew he was a new Christian but I figured he was still Derek, and so he surely must have had Los Angeles pretty well mapped out and knew where all the good times could be had.

I arranged to stay with him rather than with the band at a hotel. It was a big mistake. I knew something was wrong as soon as he picked me up. We were waiting for the garage attendant to bring up his car from the underground parking structure when, after our helloes, he said, 'Barry, there's something I've got to tell you.'

I mentally ducked, guessing he was going to heavy me with something.

'I don't know if you know it or not, but the world we live in is in a big mess and it's not going to last for ever.' His usually good-humoured face was still, serious and composed.

Momentarily nonplussed, I passed on replying, but thought to myself, 'Big deal. Just so long as it lasts as long as I'm on it.'

Derek seemed impervious to my reaction to his preaching and ploughed on:

"And whether you believe it or not Barry, one day Jesus Christ is going to return for his church.' Now he was really airborne! 'And if you're not in his church, you're going to be in big trouble.'

I realised I was already in 'big trouble'. I'd committed myself to spend a few days with a man who was obviously in need of some serious psychiatric help. If I'd have had more backbone, I would have said goodbye for ever right there and then and happily never conversed with my friend again. But I had a 'flaw' in my character of never wanting to upset anybody, so I figured I would just have to ride this one out.

Barney's Beanerie in Hollywood was a trendy hand-out for rock and rollers as well as 'wanna-be's', and this was where Derek took me one day. As I sunk my teeth into one of their famous burgers, I tried to keep the conversation off religion and magnanimously plied Derek with many questions about life in L.A. Derek received them and, for some reason, turned each answer around to having some reference to the Bible.

After an excruciatingly embarrassing journey, we arrived at Derek's home in the Hollywood Hills. He lived with a small group of other people. Surely they weren't religious nuts as well?

After a few moments of introduction, I realised from all the 'hallelujahs' and 'praise God, Brother, we're glad you're here,' that Derek was not the only one in need of help. My mood had abruptly switched to tired irritation. They were all so happy, and their joy made me somehow aware of my own distinct lack of it.

Those couple of days were worse than any chemistry class I had attended back in school in Huntingdon. In fact, they were worse than anything I'd ever endured anywhere. The people weren't pushy in trying to ram their beliefs down my throat, it was just that they *did* believe and that affected the whole way that they lived. Their relationship with Jesus Christ seemed as real and valid as any of their other relationships and it had provided them with a joy and a zest for life that made me angry.

I was even dragged along to a Bible study in a house somewhere in Los Angeles. I found it incredibly boring. The place was jam-packed with smiling Californians clutching Bibles, closing their eyes and lifting their hands and singing choruses. The house was so full that I spent the evening trying to peer through a crack in the kitchen door to catch a glimpse of the guy who was teaching from the Bible. Mind you, even I had to admit that his message was a lot more relevant and real than anything else I'd ever heard during my brief stint at church in England.

That short entanglement with Christianity had come about years before, when I had joined the Boy's Brigade. My motive was learning to play the drums, but I soon grew tired of the whole thing when I discovered that there was a pathway that had to be travelled in order to get your hands on the drumsticks. And that involved learning first to play the bugle, not exactly a rock and roll instrument.

Part of the Boy's Brigade ritual was attendance at the local Methodist church and, maybe it was just my age, but it seemed awfully boring on those Sunday mornings, the highlight of which was trying to out-shout Mr Lane, he bellowed with all of his heart the words of Wesley's hymns. He was one of the elders of the church who had a booming voice and a foot that had been run over by a tank in the Second World War.

Fortunately, the three-day nightmare in Los Angeles eventually ended and Arizona beckoned. In my heart, I knew that this was the last time I would ever see Derek again. And I was prepared to bear the bad tidings of his total insanity to all my friends in England.

As Derek dropped me off at the hotel before we left, he handed me a couple of books and said, 'I want you to take these and give them a read. They really meant a lot to me and opened up my eyes.'

I took them and glanced down at their titles. They were *Mere Christianity* by C. S. Lewis and *The Late Great Planet Earth* by Hal Lindsey.

'Thanks Derek,' I muttered, trying to be as nice as possible but, thinking all the time that if I took them he'd shut up and not embarrass me any more.

With a deep sense of relief, I boarded the tour bus and left for the sanctuary of life on the road. As we drove through the desert to Arizona, I thumbed through the books, more out of boredom than any-thing else. They weren't actually as tiresome as I thought they would be. In fact, they expressed some realities that I had never considered before. They seemed to be talking about a God who was at work in the earth, who was intimately involved with the humans on it and who, from their perspective, had a plan. I stuffed the books at the bottom of my bag and resumed my life with the band.

However hard I tried, I just couldn't leave them alone. I told myself it was because I was concerned about Derek's mental health, feeling that 'normal' people did not have to get so worked up about God and all that religious stuff. I resolved that I would make it a personal mission to disprove from the Bible what these men were saying and then prove to Derek that this Christianity business wasn't really necessary.

My assignment became all-consuming. I spent every spare moment taking these books and their references to the Bible and attempting to show the futility of their thesis. The one thing I had remembered from my English class at school was that it's very easy to take things out of context and make things say what you want, so I figured I'd put their quotes back in context and get the real picture.

Strangely enough, the more I tried to disprove one of these writers, the more I found myself agreeing with him. After a while I decided that maybe I should just forget the books and study the Bible for myself so that I could, at least, let Derek know that I'd done a good job of trying to accept what he was on about.

As the AC-DC bus traversed the nation, and as everybody else continued with their usual antics from consuming drugs to watching porno films, I ploughed through the Old Testament. I wasn't too impressed. This God seemed to wreak an awful lot of destruction, wiping out nations, killing people. I, of course, had my standard argument, 'If God is God and he is a God of love,' which Derek was continually telling me, 'then how come there is injustice and people starving?' Another was, 'How is it that evil men are triumphing over good?' 'How come there is so much suffering in the world?' And none of my Bible reading seemed to be providing any answers.

I read one day of a French philosopher, Emile Caillet, who, while sitting in the trenches during the First World War, reflected on the misery, despair and emptiness of his life and longed to find a book that, in his words, 'would understand him'. Alongside this barbed element of the 'sin issue', I began to discover that as well as highlighting my present state, it seemed that God's plan was not to leave me there but provide a remedy, a release. There was an awful lot of reading about 'sin' and God's dealing with it. The general sense coming through was a certain helplessness in mankind, a condition from which there seemed to be no hope of liberation. I certainly didn't regard myself as 'sinner' material, but something about this pricked my conscience and spoke to my condition, which was quite uncomfortable. I pressed on, though, because I was doing this for my friend.

The strange thing was that Derek had always talked to me about Jesus during our time together in Los Angeles. I knew all about Jesus because we'd studied him in school. But now, as I moved into the New Testament, the Jesus described there and the one that I thought I knew turned out to be two completely different people.

Although, on the surface, nothing was moving me, inside stuff was starting to happen. I had always been bugged by the question of 'Why are we here?' and, as

I read the Bible, it seemed to be telling me that I was here because God had a purpose in it.

But I couldn't reconcile myself to this God because of the world in which I lived. I had also always remembered a quote that we had heard in school when we had studied the Russian Revolution. Karl Marx had boldly declared that 'religion is the opiate of the masses'.

Coming from a working-class family, I found a certain appeal in the class struggle that took place in Russia; it was one of the few times that I was genuinely interested in something we studied at school. I guess, though, our British 'class struggle' was rather predictable. Voting Labour was a matter of course, regardless of the candidate. I had some friends who were involved with the young socialists, and listening to them it was easy to pinpoint and explore the oppressions and injustices of the rich and all the hypocrisy of the church. I remember, even then, understanding Marx's comment because in our town there were a few old churches. They were beautiful Gothic buildings, but somehow out of touch with life in the twentieth century.

It seemed that the church had had its day. It reached its peak when people were a little more naïve; perhaps more susceptible to fables and the concept of God. This was the space age and we needed some real answers. We didn't need to go on hobbling on the crutch of religion.

The more I read, the more I realised that the God whom I thought I knew as the God of Christianity was far removed from the God who was revealed in the pages of the Bible. I read about Jesus, I found myself on occasions really touched by his compassion and caring for ordinary people. He seemed to be for the common man and he definitely seemed to have a bee in his bonnet about suffocating, self-righteous, religious attitudes that oppressed rather than liberated.

In a few months, I got through the whole Bible. I didn't have too many answers to give Derek, but I'd certainly given myself a lot of food for my own personal thought.

After I put down my Bible, I muttered to myself, 'What about all the other religions? Well, they're all the same, aren't they?'

To make sure that they were 'all the same' I amassed an amazing assortment of books on any religion I could find and began to study them. I welcomed the approach of the people who hung out in airport terminals, donated to their cause and received with delight their books of enrichment and enlightenment, which made for strange reading. I think my friends on the road crew thought that I had smoked one joint too many and never come back.

It was actually funny, because here was this anti-Christian pseudo-intellectual poring over books on Buddhism, Hari Krishna and Islam. You name it and I found it. And I kept catching myself saying, 'Well, that's all very well, but that's not what the Bible says.' Which confused me all the more.

I came to one firm conclusion, and that was that all religions are not the same; that the choices and opinions are endless. Most of them were a little too strange even for me. So much pressure to perform; to capture the attention of 'God', whoever or whatever he might be. And there always seemed to be the threat that if I blew it in this life, I'd come back in the next as maybe an ant that somebody was going to step on, and that would be my just desserts for the life that I had led.

I came away from all this with a line drawn in my

heart knowing that there was a great difference between Christianity and all the other religions and a sense that this was a book that 'understood me', which was a little scary. That much I was prepared to concede. But where it fitted in with me I wasn't sure. I'd certainly come to an awareness that if God was real, there wasn't much I could do to impress him and, although I regarded myself as a pretty good person— after all, I'd never murdered anybody—his standard was different, unattainable apart from a relationship with Christ.

But Jesus and rock and roll didn't seem to form a strong relationship, and rock and roll I knew; Jesus I wasn't too sure about.

I asked all of my friends on our bus their opinion of Christianity. We all pretty much agreed that it was absolutely certain that we were all Christians. We were English, basically good natured with no plans to do any harm, just out to enjoy life and obviously worthy and destined to do well at the pearly gates! The best thing for me was to stop trying to be something I already was. Funnily enough though, the more we talked about it, the more it seemed that all of our opinions and prejudices were far removed from the brand of Christianity that I had discovered in the Bible.

This led to some heated discussions. Plug, an affectionate name for one of the guitar technicians, was a science fiction addict. He had his own particular assessment of God in general and the gospel in particular. It had a lot to do with aliens and creatures from other planets. It was pretty obscure, but he was convinced of his allegiance to Christianity, nonetheless.

We almost got into fist fights over the concept of a

loving God who allowed suffering in the world. A big source of conflict was the day we discussed forgiveness and whether or not God would let people like Hitler into heaven if they were truly sorry for what they had done. That discussion got so heated that it startled our driver and our bus almost ran off the road as we yelled and screamed at each other. These were heady topics to discuss in the cramped confines of a tour bus full of tired and cranky roadies.

I found myself vehemently defending the gospel, but not actually committed to it in a tangible way in my own life. Something had touched my heart and, for the first time in my life, the hard shell of anger and frustration that had encrusted my heart was beginning to peel away.

I took our conversations seriously and began to ask questions of this God that I wasn't too sure that I believed in. I was just as confused about those issues as the other guys were, but I could not buy the argument that it was okay to do what you were doing until you got older and then, when you were too decrepit to have fun any more, you became a normal Christian, stopped having fun, settled down and got married— the two went hand in hand—and went to church for Christmas and Easter. At least that seemed to be the general consensus. Something told me that there was more to it than that; that it was something that I needed to take hold of now. That maybe waiting was a dangerous thing to do.

Perhaps it was the fact that I had already experienced the death of people around me that told me that there weren't guarantees that we were all going to live to a ripe old age.

But then what?

Chapter Six

AND THE BAND PLAYED ON

As the arena lights lowered, a full-throated anticipatory roar rose from the 18,000 hard-core AC-DC fans assembled at the Kobo Arena in Detroit. That deafening wall of sound, and the sight of a thousand points of flickering light emanating from cigarette lighters throughout the indoor stadium, was an amazing experience for me, even after I had witnessed so many concerts all over the world.

Cliff Williams, who was now the band's bass player, began the intro to AC-DC's standard opener, 'Problem Child'. As his bass thumped the opening rhythm, the crowd's roar rose to a crescendo. Phil then kicked in with his bass drum, quickly followed by the combined crunching power chords of Angus and Malcolm's guitars.

A solitary spotlight picked out Bon as he launched into a primeval scream, his trademark introduction. The lights onstage then came flashing on and lit up the arena and we were off into another night of uninhibited rock and roll, circa 1979.

My sole job now with the group was to set up Phil's drums, mix the sound for his monitor system, and generally take care of his needs. Phil and I had become quite close friends and we roomed together. We had weathered a lot of situations in which I helped through periods of extreme stress on the road. He liked to be in close communication even during the concert, so I arranged the stage equipment so that I could stand less than three feet away from him throughout the concert, mix the sound, and yet not be seen by anyone.

We had been on the road for a few months, so there were few problems. Everything had settled into a well-oiled routine and was running smoothly. This was a good concert with an excited audience. It's amazing how an audience can affect the way a band plays. If the electricity is there from them, that seems to draw out the best in the band; if not a show can often go flat.

Of course, I'd heard these AC-DC songs year after year and knew every chord change and pretty much everything that would happen in the concert. They would play favourites from albums like *High Voltage*, *Let There Be Rock*, *Powerage*, *If You Want Blood, You've Got It* and *Highway to Hell*.

I glanced across the large stage to another guy who was hidden away behind Malcolm's amplifiers and speakers. He was Keith, a Brummie with a keen sense of humour.

Keith, who was Malcolm's guitar technician, appeared to have one main aim in life—to do as little as possible in the shortest amount of time and have the best fun doing it. He had managed to narrow his job down to plugging in Malcolm's speaker cables to the amplifiers, changing his guitar strings and making sure that his bar was well stocked. Not bad considering the tons of equipment we were carting around. But we could never get mad at him because he was always coming up with incredibly funny off-the-cuff remarks that would have us in stitches, and his thick Brummie accent was the source of many a good laugh as he traversed the country trying to communicate his charm to the bemused Americans.

In his little hideaway, Keith had set up his own personal pub, complete with wide selection of beverages as well as a dart board. Another one of Keith's missions in life was to chat up what he called 'sweet, shy, mysterious, girls.'

As the concert progressed, Keith lifted up a can of Coca-Cola and mouthed across the stage to me, 'Do you want it?'

'Sure,' I replied, so he ran behind the equipment and handed it to me.

I took the Coke and, as I opened it, something weird happened to me. Here I was in the middle of this concert and a thought flashed through my head: 'Barry, you've either got to forget all this God stuff and carry on with the life you're living, or stop it all and go on with God.'

I could sense the emotions lying just beneath the surface like a volcano about to erupt and, as the music receded into the background of my awareness, I reflected on the life I had been living. I came to the conclusion that I didn't particularly want to carry on in this way. In my mind's eye, I scanned the past few years of my existence and came to the conclusion that all I had done in my efforts to find answers and some kind of inner peace, had resulted in me becoming a hard-hearted, cynical, drug-wasted young man. Outwardly I was not a bad person, in fact I was generally congenial and easy to get on with, but inside a desperate person was locked away, troubled and unsettled.

The future of continuing in that life seemed quite bleak. Everything was tolerable—in fact more than that, provided I didn't examine it too closely. All at once I felt an overwhelming sense of futility and loneliness. Flocked images tumbled over one another in my mind. The one thing that I had discovered was that, for all their initial pleasures, drugs had not been that good to me. It had become more of a chore than an enjoyment now, a habit, the routine of buying, taking, getting high then coming down. My body had become wasted and I had had some close brushes with what I can only believe was death. Recently, every few months, I was having strange symptoms, almost like epileptic fits where I would lose control of my limbs and wind up shaking on the ground.

I also seemed to have a permanent cold, probably because of all the stuff I put up my nose. My stomach was always upset. To make matters worse, I was regularly coughing up blood and had a hard time eating my food.

As much as I loved music, I realised there was no redemption in it, that my heroes, the musicians of my day, the people that our generation revere and worship, didn't have any answers either. They were ordinary people, who had an extraordinary occupation and lifestyle, but they were no different from anyone else. It was that brief moment each day when they strapped on their guitars and hit the stage that their lives had anything different going on in it. We value and prize fame, but it is a strange and momentary phenomenon.

I had met a lot of great people, but no one seemed to have much of an idea of where we were going. I saw the folly of riches, the incredible lengths that people go to make it to the top and then the fickleness of humanity that leaves them next year for some other hero.

The band would sing once in a while, 'It's a long way to the top if you want to rock and roll.' It was a true statement. The whole concept of overnight success is, I think, the figment of some journalist's imagination. Quite honestly, I wondered if making it to the top had any point to it anyway. It didn't for Janis Joplin and Jimmy Hendrix.

I had rejected most of the standards of my day. I regarded them as shallow and hypocritical and I had developed my new morality, which was do your own thing and screw everybody else—as politely as possible, of course, but I was just as shallow and hypocritical.

Then there was all this God stuff. I had to come to terms with the fact that I wasn't a Christian. I may have been exposed to certain Christian ethics, but what the Bible had to say about being a Christian was far removed from what I was. And even though I still had a lot of unanswered questions, I had pretty much accepted that perhaps a lot of the problems in the world, which God got ultimate blame for, were born out of the fact that generally God wasn't invited into the situations in the first place. I'm not sure that I could lay the blame for people starving to death in India on God because I didn't see him inviting them to worship rats, which spread disease, and allowing cows to be regarded as holy animals who had the right to roam around and eat whatever they liked while people starved to death.

In some ways, I think I felt anger towards God even though outwardly I claimed no belief in him.

Maybe I was mad that I'd been born into this generation, living in a council house, flung into a world full of
potential nuclear disaster, human injustice and all the
rest of the stuff that plagues our world. And then there
was Jesus Christ who supposedly came to reveal God
to this world.

A friend of mine had once said in a discussion that
the thing that bothered him about Christianity was
that it was too simple. But maybe that was the point.
We live in such a complex world that we feel we need
incredibly complicated answers. But from what I'd
read, I had to concede that the God of the Bible
seemed to have a firm grasp on the reality of the
human condition and, on that basis, he had provided
an answer that he himself would come and live as a
man in this world and take upon himself all of the
ugliness of this world.

In that moment, as the band played on, I became
really aware of who Barry Taylor was at that moment
in time. The hypocrisies, the absolute emptiness of my
life, hit me.

'I don't want to carry on this way,' I finally
resolved, marshalling all my strength.

So really, for me at that moment, there was no
choice. I realised the beckoning of a God who, even
when we don't believe in him, is at work. Who even
when we deny his existence, has a plan and a purpose
for us being on the planet and who, in his great love,
sent his Son to save us from ourselves.

I knew that I was going to choose to give my life to
God. I wasn't sure what that meant—Billy Graham
wasn't there to tell me what to do and how to do it!
And so, with that resolution firmly set in my heart, I
prayed for the first time, 'God, please get this concert
over quickly so I can give my life to you!'

I suppose that I could have made the commitment right there and then but, for some reason, I decided to wait until after the show, and do it on the tour bus.

The concert didn't end any more quickly, but once it was over, I worked harder than I had in a long time, dismantling the equipment and carrying it outside. Once we had got all the trucks loaded, I ran onto the bus for our short journey to Chicago. There's not a great distance between these two great cities, and so we had picked up a few extra passengers. They were some of Keith's 'sweet, shy, mysterious girls' and by the time our bus pulled onto the freeway, a rip roaring party was already in full swing.

The bus's stero system was blasting rock and roll; the porno video that we'd all seen time and time again was running once more on a television set up close to the front of the bus; drinks were flowing; drugs were being consumed and a 'good time' was being had by all—except me.

In the midst of all of this I took out my Bible. I wasn't sure how I was supposed to do this. I flipped through it but that didn't seem to be making much sense. I tried to remember some prayers that we had prayed at school in our morning assemblies, and one that sprang to mind was something that our head-master recited quite often. It said, 'Teach us, good Lord, to serve thee as thou deserveth, to give and not to count the cost, to fight and not to heed the wounds, to toil and not to seek for rest, to labour and not to seek for any reward, save that of knowing that we do thy will.'

My vigil of waiting was over.

How I remembered that prayer I don't know. But somehow that night when I said it, I wasn't going through the motions as when I'd been at school making jokes and cracking up with my friends and eyeing the girls. Now it was with all my heart. After that, I said, 'God, I want the life that you have for me. Whatever it is and whatever it takes, I want to live for you in the earth. Amen!'

What came next, I wasn't sure. But I *was* sure that something was going to have to change—and soon.

Chapter Seven

MUSIC CITY BLUES

I was waiting for a pedestrian crossing light in a Nashville street to change in my favour, when a girl walked up to me and said, 'Do you know that Jesus loves you?'

'Yes, actually I do,' I said eagerly.

She seemed floored. 'You do?' she asked, amazed.

Maybe it was my appearance. Inwardly I knew I was now a follower of Jesus Christ, but outwardly I was still doing my Johnny Cash impersonation. Huntingdon's 'Man in Black' was still roaming the streets.

'You're not from around here, are you?' she said, trying to recover her composure.

'No, I'm English,' I replied, stating what I thought was the obvious.

'Are you going to school here?' she continued, repeating what seemed to be a standard question in a land where people appear to be perpetually 'going to school' for something or other.

'No, actually, I'm working for a band.'

'Oh, that's great. So you're in the ministry?'

I wasn't quite sure what she meant. I wasn't yet versed in Christian-speak.

'I think it's great that you are ministering the gospel to young people with music,' she pressed on.

'Oh, it's not a Christian band,' I said.

Her face paled. 'Oh, what is it then?'

'I'm working for AC-DC. We're in town doing a concert.'

By now she completely lost her cool and called across the street to a couple of her friends. I wasn't sure what all the fuss was about but she was convinced we needed to have a serious talk. So I put the search for drumsticks on hold for a few minutes.

I had decided not to immediately quit the AC-DC entourage because I knew if I did, this would leave them in the lurch right in the middle of a tour. Although my job was technically quite simple, it wasn't something anyone could walk straight into.

I also felt a moral obligation to stay on, figuring that if I needed this relationship with Christ, then it was an absolute certainty that my rock and roll friends did as well. And they were still my friends.

A couple of months later, during a stop in Nashville, Phil asked me to find some special drumsticks for him. I was walking through the streets of Music City USA when I ran into this group of Christians with a 'hell-fire and brimstone' posture. They were a check to me, as I had occasionally used the same presentation with the guys on the road, but generally I tried to be as non-confronting as possible, to share from my heart with them what had happened to me.

The reception I had received was generally good. Of course I was subjected to the usual 'Holy Joe' jokes. My friends had obviously noticed a change in me—and my lifestyle. Drugs had completely lost their appeal and, amazingly after so many years of constant use, the desire had gone as well. But, every once in a while, the challenge would come, 'What harm is one joint going to do you, Barry? After all, God made grass, didn't he?'

When I refused to take the marijuana, this inevitably resulted in arguments, but most of the time the band and the crew just accepted me and what I was going through. A band on the run was used to strange people coming around, so what difference did one more make?

My Bible reading had become a little more regular and I avoided a lot of situations that I would have gone into before, especially girls and drugs.

The street preachers backed me into the doorway of a closed shop and proceeded to read me the riot act. 'Don't you realise you are participating in the work of Satan?' one of them stated firmly.

'As a Christian, you have no right to be fellowshipping with sinners and being yoked with unbelievers,' said one of them, his voice dripping with contempt for the debased times he had lived to see.

My response as to why I was there fell on deaf ears and they wanted me immediately to go back to the concert hall, take my belongings off the bus and join them. I understood their concern, but even though my desires to stay may have seemed immature to them, I couldn't just leave my responsibilities until a replacement was found. I offered a dry smile and decided to say no more.

It seemed to me that God had met me in the midst of my rock-and-roll days and he hadn't shown me immediately that I needed to leave. He saved me right in the middle of it. After a few moments of eye-to-eye duelling, I said goodbye to the group.

My friendly captors finally let me go and advised me to 'get out' as quickly as I could. I left with a resolve to never condemn or prejudge human beings who are outside of the kingdom.

I cringed when we arrived at other venues and were confronted with placard-carrying protestors convinced that we were all on our way to hell. It's not that it wasn't true—I'm just not sure it was the most effective evangelistic outreach.

'If heaven's going to be populated with people like them, I think I'd rather go somewhere else,' said one of the road crew after being confronted with a group of fanatical Christians.

I recalled reading the story of a woman who had lived a sordid existence and came to Jesus with repentance and tears, much to the chagrin of the pious Pharisees. Jesus's response to their indignation was that 'those who are forgiven much love much'.

The Pharisees were consumed and upset by the woman's sinful and immoral lifestyle. Jesus was concerned about her heart and its brokenness. The Pharisees pointed out her condition. Jesus did not, but gave her the hope of freedom from that condition.

It's so easy to condemn people for the existence they are in, but the simple fact is that they are lost. They don't know. Ignorance is their guide and their blindness.

Of course, I was well aware there was another 'gospel' being preached through rock music. It was called 'sex, drugs and rock and roll are all the body needs'. Again the Bible says, 'As a man thinks in his heart, so he is.'

But Jesus never condemned blindness. Instead, he brought sight. What he did condemn were those who drove a wedge between lost men and a living God. It's very easy to condemn the world; to assign people as unsavable. To say that certain people are too far from the kingdom to ever make it in—and that seems to be a general response to many who are in the media industry, especially the hard rock and heavy metal bands.

Our task, I believe, is to shine as lights in the midst of a 'wicked and perverse generation', bringing the light of Jesus Christ to a world that cannot see. After all, we who are in the kingdom were once blind ourselves and even now we only see 'in part'.

What these Nashville street people didn't know is that God was at work with AC-DC and, even though I cannot say that any one member of the band ever came to what we call a 'saving knowledge of Christ', what the Lord had done for me brought definite circumstances to bear that allowed his name to be spoken into their world.

During the last two months of this tour, as we wound up in France, on the band's bus, the tour manager's wife (a Japanese girl and also a Christian) just happened to have with her the eight-hour version of *Jesus of Nazareth*. Bored with the daily fare of Clint Eastwood and John Wayne movies, the band watched it while travelling between shows. That got us talking.

One of the things that brought me to God was my understanding from the Bible that I had been made for a purpose and I wanted to know what that was. By the time our tour had finished, I knew that it was time to go.

I wrote a letter to Phil, the drummer, explaining as

best I could the reasons for which I was leaving and walked away from a life of rock and roll into a new life—based upon the Rock!

Chapter Eight

JOHNNY B. LOVE

I knew two Christians in the world, Derek and my grandmother. No offence to Grandma, but I opted for Derek. It seemed that we shared much more in common. So, after a brief stay at home with Pete and my other friends, who had also amazingly in their own ways begun their own individual examination of this whole Christianity thing, I decided to go to Los Angeles for a while so that my new life had a chance to grow, and to discover the plan that God had for my life.

Derek picked me up at Los Angeles International Airport in his trusty Dodge Dart and took me to his home that not long before had been such a house of horrors.

'Mate, I never thought I'd be back here again with you and your crazy friends,' I smiled.

Derek seemed to think it was pretty inevitable and told me of the many hours of prayer that had gone up for me and all the gang in Huntingdon.

'It's really quite amazing how God brought me to

America so that I could become a Christian, and how that has affected all of our lives,' he said warmly.

When we arrived at Derek's home, I was warmly welcomed by the others living there. This time I felt as though I was among family.

Derek was in a Christian band called Ark, which was more related to 'ark the 'erald angels sing than to Noah's boat. Ark were playing in churches around Southern California and all of the group were living at Derek's house.

So even though I had left the music business, I was still involved in many ways and began to help the group with their equipment and sound. I was also eagerly anticipating getting involved in his church. I felt the need to understand all of this stuff and I wanted to expose myself as much as possible to people who had insight to what God was saying to our generation.

The Bible study that they had taken me to on my previous visit had now blossomed into a church called Glendale Christian Center, which Derek attended. It was full of an interesting cross-section of people, old and young, from all walks of life.

Pastor Rick was instrumental in helping me get established in my relationship with God. Many of those in the church were like me, fairly new to the faith, which made me feel very comfortable as I struggled to come to terms with taking on the character and lifestyle of Jesus.

Rick had a real burden for different nations of the earth and consequently we were often treated to visits by missionaries from various countries around the globe. Since becoming a Christian, the whole issue of the world I lived in had become of great concern to me. I had always loved to travel, but now I felt God had a message that the whole world needed to hear.

Most of the missionaries that came were pretty ordinary people who, in obedience to God, had embarked on incredible adventures. One man had started a whole series of orphanages throughout Brazil, when most other people were thinking about their retirement. He'd lived in Brazil for many years, but still hadn't mastered the language. He couldn't preach very well and was still as American as apple pie, and yet God had blessed his meek heart and compassion for the countless, parentless children in the cities of Brazil.

These missionaries spoke to my heart about how God wants to touch the world with his gospel, and how that can be achieved by ordinary people who have come to faith in Christ and then live their lives wholly for him.

I was determined to discover God's purpose for me. I still had no idea what it was, but I was determined to find it out. There were a few things which began to fall into place. As I've said, I've always had this travel bug, but when I'd got to places, I was never satisfied by just looking around. Something in me felt there was work to be done, but I had no idea what it was.

One of the hardest lessons I had to learn was the whole concept of living in one place for an extended period. Things change when you live somewhere and you don't just breeze into town in your bus and leave again a few hours later. I began to learn that the relationship vertically with God was generally easy; it was the horizontal relationships that tested the reality of what I claimed to believe.

I also quickly realised that, while I was still new to the faith, I prided myself on having all the answers. It was so much easier to set other people straight than to remove the 'logs' in my own eye. But God is gracious and merciful and he worked in me. I began to grow in grace, and my life as a Christian began to take shape.

I must admit that after the constant excitement of life on the road, this existence was, by comparison, generally mundane. But I experienced a peace that I'd never known before and I've since come to learn that our relationship with God is cemented and strengthened as we walk with him in our day-to-day existence.

Although my heart was concerned for my growth in God, I must be honest and say that one of the things that kept me going back to the church was a girl that I met the first night.

Cathy was an incredibly vibrant person with beguiling green eyes and long raven hair. I had never met anyone so full of life—not in an overpowering way, but just in the smile on her face and her glow. I soon discovered the reason for Cathy's zeal for life and her bubbly effervescent personality. She had, at one point, been terminally ill with a disease that affected her central nervous system and she became literally allergic to the twentieth century. Things that you and I ignore were perils to her very existence. Modern-day chemicals and plastics assaulted her body until she reached a point where she was confined to an isolated environment, completely locked away from the world, unable even to read the Bible because the smell of the ink would make her incredibly sick.

Cathy spent almost four years in that hell, quite a contrast from her prior career as a top model in L.A.

She had shrunk down to 4½ stone, lost all of her hair and hadn't walked for years. Yet here she was now, in church, living in the real world, fine and healthy again.

It was now easy to understand Cathy's relationship with God and the high value she placed on life. In fact, one of the lessons that I learned from her was that life is much too precious to take for granted. She had experienced all that the world had to offer, and had dated many well-known personalities including Robert Plant, lead singer with Led Zeppelin. She had even been at the recording of the classic *Stairway to Heaven*. But now she had discovered the true stairway to heaven.

After a couple of months of quick helloes and snatched glances during the service, Cathy walked up to me one day after church for a chat. I later discovered that she was interested in me but had resolved that she wasn't ready for any relationship as she had recently gone through the pain of breaking up with someone else. Still, for some reason, she felt an attraction. Cathy came up to me fully expecting me to open my mouth and be an absolute wally so that she could write it off and go on with her life. But she didn't bargain on the English accent—and so our relationship blossomed!

We did the usual Christian dating thing—as many Bible studies as possible, purely a backdrop for our growing love for each other. Cathy's high regard for life really made me consider the waste of my own so far.

Here was someone who had fought so desperately to live, while I, in many ways, had been on a path of self-destruction, abusing my body and taking it for granted. Cathy had also, because of the nature of her illness, had to deal with many of her own personal idiosyncrasies. Being a model, she had prided herself on her appearance, in fact made a living from it, and confessed to the fact that a broken finger nail could ruin her whole day. But being confined to a room and having her looks disappear day by day had taught her a deep lesson. Now she had an incredible burden for people to cut through shallow things. She had experienced the pain of people not wanting to come and visit her because they would have to come without their make-up or hairspray. Or people just calling her on the telephone and gossiping and back-biting their so-called friends.

All this had birthed a desire and a determination in Cathy to see God's people come to a place where they never took their relationship with God and each other for granted.

I liked that a lot.

Our blossoming love for each other led to a mutual decision to get wed, and after a bungled attempt to get married in England due to immigration problems, we wound up in The Little Church of the West in Las Vegas on a crazily hot day in August, joined in holy matrimony by the Reverend Johnny B. Love, who assured us that that was his real name.

Not long after leaving the band came the tragic news that AC-DC vocalist Bon Scott had died from choking on his vomit after an all-night drinking binge. It was a ridiculous end to a life and such a waste. Bon was a really nice guy with a great heart. He was always amiable and unaffected. I hoped the discussions we had had about Christ and his viewing of the *Jesus of Nazareth* videos had touched him inside.

I reflected on where all this success had led such a talented singer. And I thought on the irony of an album called *Highway to Hell* becoming a platinum hit.

Chapter Nine

THE HANDS OF THE BODY

I hadn't bargained on living in America, and Los Angeles would certainly never have been my first choice. But Cathy wasn't yet ready to pack up and move to jolly old England. Having grown up in Southern California, the prospect of living in the fens of East Anglia during a biting winter was none too appealing.

I really loved England. However, I think at that stage in my life, it would have been detrimental for me to return home. I needed the freshness that life in California seemed to offer. If we English suffer from too much cynicism and negativity, California provides the balance of wide-eyed acceptance of just about everything.

Having grown up a closet cynic, I needed a healthy dose of American 'you can do it if you really want to' mentality. We reached a compromise. Cathy had a weekend cabin in a place called Lake Arrowhead, which is a resort area in the San Bernardino Mountains, a couple of hours south of L.A.

On a visit there, as we drove along the mountain's

edge and through the pine forests, I told her that I thought I could handle living up there.

'It will be a struggle, but I think I could make it,' I told her, tongue firmly in cheek.

It was a beautiful spot, known locally as Little Switzerland. There were no Alps, but plenty of snow for skiing all year round, which is unusual in Southern California.

The road up the mountain is called Rim of the World Highway, and I liked that. It seemed to have a prophetic quality to me and it was up there on the mountain top that Cathy and I started our life together and God began to lay out his purpose for us.

One of the things that I had read in the Bible which immediately struck me was God's obvious plan to include all the nations on the earth and, of course, Jesus' mandate to his disciples before his ascension to 'go into all the world and preach the gospel'. My desire to travel didn't waver when I gave my life to Christ, but in many ways intensified. Here was a reason beyond new sights and cultures to discover; there were lives like mine that needed to hear the call and love of God.

I had begun to intercede daily for the nations of the earth and one day, in prayer, it suddenly occurred to me to pray for the Soviet Union. I came to an abrupt halt: quite honestly, I didn't know what to pray. It was a Communist nation that advocated atheism as an ideology and lifestyle. I had heard that Christianity had been stamped out and that, rather than pining for heaven, the socialists had achieved 'heaven on earth' and didn't need what they considered to be the 'fairy tale' of religion.

I then began to consider all the other countries on the earth that had turned their backs on God, or who had their own particular belief about who God was. But my heart kept coming back to the Soviet Union. I wondered if God had a plan for Russia, and I had to believe that he did because my reading of the Bible told me that he loved the whole *world* so much that he gave his only begotten Son.

Jesus didn't come just for the Western nations, but for the whole earth. And Jesus had committed the carrying of his gospel to his church. What a wild concept; that God would entrust such an incredible message to people like me!

The challenge of taking that 'good news' to the nations of the earth began to take a hold of me. We live in a world of incredible opportunity. Fifty years ago, much of what went on in the world took for ever to become global news. Now, on a daily basis, the world is dumped unceremoniously into our living rooms, and events on the other side of the globe become common knowledge moments later. Through satellite communication we have become a global village.

And what a world we live in. So much incredible pain and suffering. In some ways, I think all that information has cauterised our hearts. We are so used to seeing people blown up, maimed and killed, and in varying states of decay in the protected environments of our living rooms that it's almost become unreal.

We have more people living on this planet than ever before, more of them in Second and Third World nations, born into hardship and suffering. It's our task as Christians to bring to them the gospel, the only real hope.

Initially, my response to all this was, 'What can I do?' However, the more I studied my Bible, the more it seemed to me that God has called each of us to a portion of his purpose for mankind. If we each do our little bit, the whole job can and will get done.

One of the major lessons I have learned during my life as a Christian is this whole idea of God using ordinary people. It used to be that when I read about the great men and women of faith, I would look at them as one-dimensional heroes, faster than a speeding bullet, able to leap tall buildings, to take on whole nations single-handed.

That may be Hollywood's idea of a hero, but not God's. His word is full of great men and women who lied, stole, killed, murdered, committed adultery and generally blew it—and yet his hand was upon them and he moulded them to become the men and women that he had ordained them to be.

I realised that God is not looking for perfect people, just those willing to yield their lives to his control. To let him make them into people through whom he can pour his life and love to a dying world. I read of men and women in past generations who had made an incredible impact in their lifetimes, because they simply chose to surrender their lives completely to God. Gladys Aylwood, known as the 'small woman', was rejected as a missionary candidate and yet was used by God in China. David Livingstone, committed not only to discover the source of the Nile, but also to making Christ known in Africa. Countless men and women, not necessarily of great importance or renown in their society, were ready to be transformed by him into heroes of the faith.

I read one day in the book of Acts about King David. There it declared that David, after he had served his generation in the will of God, fell asleep and went to be with his fathers. God is looking, I believe, for people willing to 'serve their generation in the will of God'.

I became absorbed with the Soviet Union and whether or not God had his hand on that vast, mysterious nation. I found some information about the conditions of the believers there and was surprised to discover that there was a healthy, though intensely repressed, body of Bible-believing Christians in that land.

The more data I uncovered, the more responsibility I felt as part of the global body of Christ, to do whatever I could to strengthen and affirm these brothers and sisters living under such conditions.

I read Paul's letter from Corinth to Rome in which he wrote, 'We being many are one body.' I realised one of the realities of being in the kingdom of God is that you are a part of a kingdom that is found in every nation of the earth. We are joined by a relationship in Christ to men and women from every tongue and nation.

While we are equally Christians, our opportunities for living out our faith are varied. We in the West are free to worship as we choose, but that's not the case for the majority of the church of Jesus Christ. Something like two-thirds of the Christians of this world live under restrictions of their beliefs and practices.

This statistic burned in my heart. I had to see for myself how believers fared in a land that denied the existence of God. I wanted to do whatever I could to aid them. That was the basis for my first trip to the Soviet Union.

I certainly don't consider myself a hero of the faith in any way, but something inside compelled me to go. I studied the basics of the Russian language and, after much prayer, took my first trip 'behind the curtain'. I carried just a few Russian Bibles with me. I had heard stories of people driving trucks across the border with thousands of Bibles inside and I commended them for that, but I knew I wasn't ready for that kind of adventure.

I flew to Moscow Airport with my friend, Ed, and there discovered that even a babe in the faith can experience the delivering power of God. I knew the Russian authorities weren't too keen on religious literature crossing their borders, so even my small amount of Bibles would be considered illegal contraband. I was a great man of faith until our plane descended onto Soviet soil, then Barry Taylor metamorphosed into a man of sweat and trepidation.

I went through panic, anxiety, and every emotion known to man. I even looked for a bathroom at the airport, not so much for myself, but for a place to dump the Bibles. But then, I thought, 'If God has brought me here, then surely he'll protect me.'

Immediately, things happened that on reflection I can only say were God's way of showing me his sovereignty over a difficult situation. We had stopped briefly in Helsinki to transfer to our Aeroflot flight directly into Moscow, the holy city of the Soviet empire. The changeover was only twenty minutes and somehow, in the rush, our luggage didn't make the flight.

At Moscow, we were informed that we couldn't pass through customs until our luggage arrived and we had declared our belongings. It was to be five hours before the next flight arrived from Helsinki, so there we were, left to wait in the customs hall. I took the opportunity to 'spy out the land' and see which of the customs officials appeared to be the most lenient.

I helped an old lady take her bags up to one official

and nonchalantly watched the proceedings. He opened all of her suitcases and even made her empty her purse and all her pockets, and then proceeded to conduct an intense search of her person. I figured this was not the man to take my belongings to when they finally arrived!

Unfortunately, the rest of the officers did exactly the same, and I began to wonder just how I was going to get myself and these few Bibles into the country. Thoughts of an extended stay in the Gulag began to permeate my mind. I battled between moments of great faith and of intense fear, convincing myself that I was an absolute idiot for being there in the first place. I knew by the perspiration knotted on my brow that I wasn't cut out for this kind of adventure.

As I watched person after person go through customs, I saw them experience the same ritual of having their belongings and their person completely searched. I had heard of people praying every time they crossed a Communist border that God would make the Bibles invisible. At that moment I was praying that God would make me invisible.

Finally our bags arrived and with hesitation I picked one of the customs officials and committed my life into the hands of the Almighty.

I figured the best approach was the friendly English tourist—'I'm so glad to be here' type of stuff. But my smiles met stony stares and a simple demand for my passport.

After studying it, the official looked at me, and said, 'Do you have any literature?'

'What do I say now?' I thought.

But he wasn't finished. '...in your suitcase,' was the end of his sentence.

'No,' I almost yelled. Of course, I didn't tell him

that there was literature in my pockets. He didn't ask me that.

The man seemed satisfied, stamped my passport, welcomed me to the Soviet Union and waved me through. No search of my person or my belongings. It was unbelievable! Hour after hour I'd watched everyone else being checked, yet here was I with a few Bibles, precious to God's people there, and God saw to it that I got through.

Once inside the country, I faced another challenge. In a nation of 286 million people, I didn't know anyone. And I figured that you didn't just walk up to people and ask if they were Christians. But again, when we give our lives to God, sometimes not even knowing exactly where we are going, God has a way of orchestrating situations that lead to divine encounters.

I visited a large official church in Moscow and, after the service, a man came up to me, obviously aware that I was a foreigner. After a brief discussion, he gave me some names of believers in the cities that I told him I was planning to visit.

These contacts led me to a small village in the Ukraine, close to a city I was visiting. I had spent the evening calling on many different groups, assembled around the area. The meetings were all 'secret' and held in homes. I had expected something very different. To me a secret meeting is one where outsiders don't know what you're doing, but this hardly seemed secret to me, as I walked through a tired and beat-up neighbourhood in the fading evening light, up to a house that was filled with about 100 believers singing their heart out. You could hear them three blocks away!

The reception we received was always incredible.

Russian bear-hugs, kisses on the cheeks and smiles and flowing tears of joy that we had come to visit them. It's an amazing experience to be jammed into a small house with a group of believers whose daily life is a constant struggle, whose leaders, because of their illegal activities, were under constant threat of disruption and imprisonment.

And yet etched on their faces was not fear, but a deep peace.

It was also phenomenal when the leaders called for prayer and, as one, all the people fell to their knees, not in ritual, but in genuine reverence for God. It was an incredible privilege to be able to bring, in broken Russian, some words of encouragement and hope to these men and women who pay such a high price for their relationship with God.

After each meeting, someone would take me to the next one by bicycle, or in a car, and so we wound up late one evening, in an old, ramshackle house on the edge of farmland, many miles from the city.

When we got to the house, we were led into the 'living room' which was bare except for a few rows of rough, wooden benches and a table which I took to be the pulpit.

Ed and I sat there in silence for quite some time, with no one but the driver for company. After a while some more people arrived, and over a period of about an hour the room gradually filled up with poor and shabbily-dressed people, none of whom said a word to me.

Finally two men came into the room. By the attention paid to them I surmised that they were the leaders. They were dressed in dirty, grimy suits, Russian sandals (cheap and made out of rubber) and what I took to have been once-white shirts.

I jumped as the silent group suddenly erupted into praise to God and expressions of obvious happiness. Everyone began to surround us, covering us both with kisses and hugs. Once they had settled down, the two men introduced themselves to me as Gennady and Shura. I understood they were the pastors of not only this assembly, but four or five others in the area. There was much rejoicing because Shura had only one month before been released from prison. He had been arrested while preaching at one of the home churches and for that had spent three years separated from his family and friends in a cruel labour camp.

The pastors had experienced an incredible amount of harassment and persecution, and they told me not to be surprised if this meeting was not disrupted by the KGB. This did wonders for my sense of security. To me, it was a very unsettling thing to hear; to them it was par for the course, part of the price that they were willing to pay for walking with God.

I had the opportunity of sharing some scriptures with them. I felt totally inadequate to do such a thing. What had I to say to men and women who obviously had a faith that was much more tried and tested than my own? But for them, the simple fact that someone from the other side of the world was there in their midst made it all worth while.

Their love and generosity was overwhelming. After a time of talking together and praying, they brought in a small tray with a plate of food, mostly potatoes with a little gravy on top, a fairly old apple and a cup of Russian tea. It was for us. Although we protested, they insisted that we eat while they watched. Having seen the lack of food in the Soviet Union, the long lines for meagre supplies, I could only think that we were eating all the food they had.

To make matters twice as hard, they then proceeded to serenade us with some incredibly moving Russian hymns, one of which was conveying the sentiment of God's protection and love until we met in heaven. It brought tears to my eyes, and as I looked around the room, the sight of all these simple but inspiring people, worshipping God with all their hearts, was almost too much for me to handle.

Shura, the most vocal of the bunch, had asked me a question that night that I'd heard before, but coming from the lips of a man who had been in prison for his faith, it seemed to carry more weight.

'It's been over fifteen years since anyone from the West has come to visit us, brother,' he said almost reflectively. 'Are we forgotten?' His eyes, dark and penetrating, peered out intently.

I assured him that they were not forgotten; that many people throughout the world prayed for them daily and stood with them in their times of trouble. I also made him a promise, one I wasn't sure I knew how to keep, to do everything within my power to ensure they never would be forgotten.

Also in the house group was an old man. He had a classic Russian face, with bushy eyebrows and a large shock of pure white hair. A hard life had left its mark over not only his face, but all of his body.

He was accorded great respect by all in the group. They told me that he had suffered much in his life for God, having come to Christ as a young boy not long after the 1917 revolution. That decision had cost him dearly, and his life since then had been a constant stream of harassment, imprisonment and hardship. Under his arm he carried a little bag which he opened to show me his greatest joy. It was a Bible that he told me had been given to him many years before by a man from Canada. Tears filled his eyes as he touched the pages and thanked God for the richness of his word.

With his age-softened hands holding mine in a grip that was firm and strong, he looked me in the face with tears rolling and said, 'Three years ago, God told us in prayer that two young men from the West would be coming to us. Every day since then we have prayed and asked God that today would be the day, and today God has answered our prayer, and you are here!'

I grabbed hold of my dear Russian brother and in Russian style kissed him on the lips, and then promptly broke into tears. I don't know if they were supposed to wait three years for the answer to that prayer. All I can say is it was a life-changing experience to stand in front of this man and to be the answer to his prayer.

I had trouble sleeping that night back in the relative comfort of my hotel room. The faces I had seen and the stories I had heard in the past few weeks had revolutionised my life for ever.

On my last day in the Soviet Union, I got up early. I was back in Moscow; our hotel was less than a quarter of a mile from Red Square. I decided to go out for an early-morning walk. The streets were just beginning to fill with people going off to work. The trucks that spray the streets with water everywhere in the Soviet Union had just been by, and that fresh, clean smell that comes just after it has rained filled the air.

As I left the long prospect and entered Red Square, I saw a huge line of pilgrims made up of all the various races of the Soviet Union; Armenians; Georgians; Mongolians with their bright-coloured, Gypsy-type clothes; Russians; and Muslims from Soviet Central

Asia; all standing patiently and with obvious excitement, waiting to catch a glimpse of their entombed saint, Vladimir Ilyich Lenin, founder of the Soviet Republic.

This long human column led across Red Square, ran down a gentle slope beside the Historical Museum, turned a corner through iron gates, passed the eternal flame for the Unknown Soldier, and rambled on for nearly a hundred yards before it dribbled away in the gardens beneath the towering fortress walls of the Kremlin.

Red Square is an imposing place. It has the Kremlin on one side, the famous GUM department store opposite, the Lenin Museum with its snow-white roof and the chaotic beauty of St Basil's Cathedral with a kaleidoscope of colours exploding on its onion-, pineapple- and cone-shaped domes. It was once the centre of Christian worship in Russia, but now a museum to a bygone age.

I stood in the square watching the citizens patiently waiting to view Lenin in the low, sober, unembellished, rectangular, red-granite 'sepulchre'. I saw mothers cautioning their children to be quiet and felt the sense of reverence that overtook the people as they got closer to the entrance of the mausoleum.

I reflected on my trip here, what it had meant to me and what it had done to me.

First, it had made me aware of the incredible gift that liberty is and how easily it is abused and taken for granted. Even the apostle Peter, in one of his letters, had cautioned the church not to take its liberty for granted and use it for their own gain, but rather take that liberty and use it as a bondservant of God. My heart was pricked. The Bible speaks of God as a redeemer of time and, although I was aware of God's forgiveness towards me, I once again repented of the waste of my life, the unnecessary, selfish, 'what a drag life is' mentality that had plagued me for so long. All this I was seeing now made my life in Huntingdon a kingly existence in comparison. When had I ever had to line up for bread, go without so many things, be told how and what to think?

Secondly, and perhaps more importantly, was that concept of the global body, members one of another. And as I stood there that day, it occurred to me that perhaps we in the West in the perspective of the global body of Christ might be the hands. Our hands are free. We are not bound, or shackled, by the imposition of ideologies and governments that restrict our worship. We are free to worship as we choose and when we choose. We can travel freely, and do so many things that the bulk of believers in the Soviet Union were not then able to do. And though Russia may relax in some respects, there are still many nations— communist, Muslim and others—where religious liberty is little more than a dream.

I decided against joining the line of pilgrims waiting to look at the body of a man long gone, and left the square resolved to carry out of the country with me not a picture of a man who had caused so much hardship and destruction, but rather the memories of men and women whose lives had challenged me to consider how I should live for God in the light of the incredible opportunity extended to me.

Could I ever be the same again?

Chapter Ten

ROMANIA'S CROSS

The voice on the phone line was to the point. 'Five o'clock on the bench opposite the tram station in the town square. Good-bye.' With that the phone went dead.

James Bond material, I thought. The voice was that of a man that my friend Dusty, a California Christian, and myself were to meet. We were in Timisoara, a city in the Socialist Republic of Romania, in the mysterious region of Transylvania, on the Yugoslav border. (It was two years yet before the incredible revolution was to begin in this very city.)

At that time, Romania was a country whose 23.5 million people were both physically and spiritually oppressed by the Marxist-Leninist regime of President Nicolae Ceausescu, whose communism was both unreconstructed and unapologetic.

It is a land which lies in south-eastern Europe, bordered to the north and north-east by the USSR, to the east by Hungary, to the south-west by Yugoslavia, and to the south by Bulgaria.

This was two years after my trip to the Soviet Union, but Romania was very different from its large neighbour. In fact it was a place which *glasnost* (openness) and time had passed by. Ceausescu, who presided over a Stalin-era economic autarky, had been openly critical of *glasnost*, and believed the only way for Romania to go was towards pure Communism. He made little secret of the fact that he wanted to close all churches in Romania and create an atheist society like that in severely repressed Albania. And this is despite the fact that most of its inhabitants professed Christianity.

Dusty and I got to the square early. We had no idea what our contact looked like, but we figured he'd find us. After all, we stuck out like sore thumbs. Trying to make ourselves inconspicuous, we had taken our oldest, most out-of-date clothing, but still managed to look incredibly stylish among the typically Eastern-bloc style of dress, which we judged to be of the early forties.

Romania is an amazing country of incredible contrasts. Huge factories suddenly appear in the middle of agricultural areas spewing their poisonous smoke over the countryside. On occasions, we drove through some pretty wild air that made even the smog of L.A. seem quite pleasant.

Travelling in our rented Romanian car was another experience, as we had to contend not only with the erratic driving style of the Romanians (drive as fast as possible and then brake at the last possible moment) but also with horses and carts loping along the highways.

I was visiting another communist-bloc nation in an attempt to be 'the hands of the body' as best I could. I had picked Romania mainly because of the stories that I had heard concerning the plight of believers there and the way many of their churches had been bulldozed.

Going to the Soviet Union had prepared me somewhat for life behind the Iron Curtain, but even that had not fully primed me for life, or should I say existence, in Romania, which has a standard of living so low that it is only beaten by Albania. It seemed as though the whole country was covered with a thick blanket of oppression and depression. No one made eye contact on the streets, and soldiers were everywhere. The shops were almost completely devoid of goods; in fact these shops made the Russian stores seem well stocked in comparison.

In the Soviet Union, the Socialist government guaranteed their people at least bread on a daily basis, yet here in what was once the bread basket of Europe, no such guarantees were made. We became accustomed to seeing a glum queue of people waiting outside stores, and then see the same queue five or six hours later just as long. What they were queuing for was a mystery to me, as the country had little available because of its draconian rationing of food.

Electricity was off for long periods of time, hot water was a rarity.

The oppressive government had a great resistance to the cause of Christianity, and yet God's hand was so obviously at work. Romania has some of the largest churches in all of Europe, both east and west. In fact, the Second Baptist Church in Oradea is the largest Baptist church in Europe and was one of the churches that Billy Graham preached in during his historic eleven-day preaching mission to Romania in September 1985. Billy Graham was the first American evangelist to be allowed into the country since the

Communist Revolution in 1944. All the pews had been cleared from the sanctuary and some 7,000 people stood and listened to the gospel being clearly presented, and an additional 36,000 milled around the church outside, listening through loudspeakers.

Among the Christians we met, we discovered an incredible resolve and seemingly indomitable spirit. The constant threat of arrest and imprisonment seemed to inspire them to do more for Christ, and perhaps in response to their zeal and obedience to the Great Commission in their nation, God was blessing.

'Hello, brothers, I'm Daniel,' were the words that greeted us as this tall, handsome, young Romanian man sat down on the bench beside us.

'Are we okay here?' I asked, squinting in the bright sunlight and wondering if we weren't a little too visible.

'We are fine. At least for a while, anyway.' His face broke into a gentle smile.

Daniel was from Cluj-Napoca, another town. He was a pastor, an evangelist, a church planter and a conference speaker, as well as an organiser of secret meetings. He turned out to be made of tempered steel, burning with a fire for God to bring his bright light to this drab country.

Daniel was thrilled we were there, mainly because we were younger and his great burden was for the youth of his generation. We asked him what his needs were.

'Our most important need is prayer,' he responded in fluent English. 'And then we need materials and "bodies" from the West to come and teach us and train us to reach our nation.'

Again, I wondered what we could possibly offer a man upon whose life God so obviously had his hand, but he seemed to think that we in the West also had much to offer. The apostle Paul said, 'Can the eye say to the hand, I have no need of you?' God has implanted graces throughout his church.

Our conversation then turned to the subject of persecution.

'There *is* persecution,' he admitted. 'Quite often I am picked up by the Securitate (Romania's ubiquitous and brutal secret police at that time) and taken to the station and questioned for a few hours. Usually they just harass me, but every once in a while I get beaten as well. Generally, however, their tactic is to wear us down by constant harassment.

'They plant people in our services to cause disruption. They spread evil rumours about us and try to cause divisions and factions, but we have learned the answer to this is to fall on our faces before God and find his peace, his strength and his refreshment.

They even bulldoze our churches to the ground, but we then meet on the rubble, and that allows our praise to the Most High to permeate the neighbourhood. So in some ways, they aid us in our evangelistic efforts.

'I would love to live in freedom,' he added, 'but for me, for now, it's not to be. The cross we must bear in Romania is one that includes suffering and hardship, and we will gladly bear it.

'Our great concern is for our brothers and sisters in the West whose cross is different, whose cross is perhaps too much freedom and materialism, and we pray for you that you will take what God has given you and use it to his glory to help not only believers in Romania, but to carry the gospel to the ends of the earth.'

I was stunned to learn that they were praying for us.

Daniel's family, his parents and his three brothers were all actively involved in Christ's mission in Romania. He bade us farewell as he left for yet another secret meeting in a town a few miles away. His parting words were, 'Don't forget us in Romania, and pray that God continues to use us in our land.'

There was a strong witness for Christ in Timisoara, and that night we gathered in a church packed with 2,000 of these precious believers. During the service, Dusty and I brought greetings from the West.

Technically it was against the law for foreigners to preach in Romanian churches, but we were allowed to bring greetings. These could be quite creative at times. We could bring greetings from the West, from America, from England, from our home church, from ourselves, from the Old Testament saints, the apostle Paul, and even read the wonderful greetings those saints of old gave!

Our interpreter, one of the elders in the church, interpreted our words and then, under his breath, whispered to me, 'Keep going, brother. Don't stop. Preach the word.'

Romans 1:8 was both my greeting and Paul's, thanking God for all of them because their 'faith is known in all the earth'. It was amazing what just being there did for these believers. It somehow brought hope and encouragement to their hearts to know that they weren't alone in the battle.

After half an hour's 'greeting' we sat down and enjoyed the vibrant service of testimony, worship and preaching that followed.

Afterwards our interpreter invited us to his home. He was yet another inspiring man of God who, although he had little to share materially, was glad to give us everything. We had a wonderful evening of prayer and fellowship with this man and his wife. His love for God was obvious through everything he said. Once again, we heard the stories of harassment and persecution, the cost of following Christ in this land, but not once, from anyone in this country, did we hear or sense any bitterness or regret towards God or for their decision to follow Christ. That, in itself, was another challenge to us who so easily lose our patience with God when his answer to our every prayer is not 'yes' or immediate.

We asked our brother what his needs were. 'For me personally, I simply ask for prayer, that God would continue to use me,' he said. 'For our church, we need reading materials, especially for our young. It's impossible to find Sunday School materials, or children's Bibles.'

And then, leaning across the table and fixing his piercing eye on mine, he said, 'There *is* something else. It's not for my church, but for another church in this town—a big church.' He obviously didn't think that his 2,000-member church was that big.

'Come back to my house tomorrow at six o'clock. I want to show you something.'

We dutifully returned the next day, wondering what it was that he wanted to show us. He drove us through the town and into another neighbourhood, and came to a halt in a cloud of dust. He parked his car on a street outside a nondescript building.

'I don't really know why I'm even bringing you here,' he said. 'I don't know what you can do and, if all you can do is pray, then that will be enough.'

We walked up the stairs of this building and then through its door. We soon discovered that the front of the building was all that remained and that, behind it, construction was going on.

It was a church, and apparently this particular group of believers, after many years of fighting with the authorities, had finally received permission to build.

'This is a great victory,' he said. 'Not just for these people but for all of us here in Romania. Generally, the authorities tear down our buildings, but because God is sovereign, they have granted permission to build and this church will become a beacon in this city to the glory of God.'

The sanctuary was in the early stages of construction, but from the framework I could see it was obviously going to be a large structure.

'It's already too small,' our friend told us. 'And when God brings the harvest, who knows where they will put the new believers? But for all of us here, it's a symbol of hope and victory.'

We were introduced to the pastor of the church who, along with many of its members, was engaged in the building process. We found out that permission to build was only the first of many hurdles. Next came the problem of finding materials to build with and, again, finding the finances to purchase those scarce items.

Dusty and I both wished we had the money right there and then to give them to build that church, but we both committed our hearts to pray and stand with them as they worked.

When it came time for us to leave Romania, we were a little concerned, as we had taken a video camera with us into the country. We had shot a lot of film not only of the country, but also of some of the saints we had met, and we had recorded dialogue.

Remembering my departure from the Soviet Union, we decided that the best approach was to run down our batteries and hope that even if they did stop us, they would have no idea exactly what it was that we had.

Dusty was an electronics buff and had also brought a pocket television with him so that he could monitor his camera work. That proved to be our ace card.

The guards at Bucharest Airport stopped us and were very interested in our camera and, once again, I thought that maybe I was going to be subjected to a strip search. But then they came across the television, they asked Dusty what it was.

Dusty decided the best thing to do was to demonstrate this pocket-sized wonder, and suddenly their surly authoritarian manner dissolved into childish curiosity as they laughed at the genius of Japanese technology.

I can only believe that God was on our side. Often, during my time on the road, I had wondered just exactly what I could possibly do that would top all of my experiences working in the rock-and-roll industry. After all, working for a band is not your average nine-to-five job, and although it's very hard work at times, it has more than its share of exciting moments. The excitement of a crowd building up before the band hits the stage, the initial blast of music and lights that erupt in your senses, the exotic locales, the general glamour of the job, all combine to make it a very desirable and fulfilling occupation.

But none of those moments could surpass the sense of being in God's plan for my life and walking with the Creator, and certainly none of those times had the lasting effect on my life that incidents like this in Romania had on me. Here I found myself in situations where there was no way out but for the help of God.

I've discovered now that the most exciting thing of

all is when men and women surrender their lives to God, and the God of heaven and earth begins to work in them, for his own good pleasure.

Romania has now finally got rid of its cruel dictator. The church there now has freedom, and a new start. Are we ready to help them with our prayers, aid and support?

Chapter Eleven

IN THE FOOTSTEPS OF DAVID LIVINGSTONE

The crowd began to sway from side to side as they chanted, 'Dumasami, hallelujah!' ('Praise God, hallelujah!') 'Dumasami, hallelujah!'

The chant became a roar as voice after voice followed the leading of the Burning Sisters, five girls who led the singing from the platform of Luveve Township Hall, a suburb of Bulawayo, Zimbabwe. Within minutes, the whole building began to resound as 700 voices combined to praise their God in a way only Africans can.

Once the hymn was completed—some thirty minutes later—the Burning Sisters did a special number with African choreography that set the place on fire. They began to sing a song in their Matabele dialect and soon were joined by the whole congregation who instinctively followed the dance steps. It wasn't long before two stiff white men on the stage joined the sisters in their steps.

You could never get depressed in an African

church; just the simple joy of their worship is enough to change even the hardest cynic's heart.

As I sat on the stage during that service in November 1989, I thought back to a visit I had made with a colleague during the afternoon to a small village about twenty miles from town. As we drove with Samuel Mahbena, our local contact, along the bouncy, dusty road, we passed a building with a simple wooden sign on the outside which said it all: 'David Livingstone Mission.'

About 150 years prior, a man who became one of the world's most famous explorers and missionary statesmen began the work of bringing light to what was then regarded as the 'Dark Continent'. Words had changed David Livingstone's life. As a man already committed to Jesus, he was prepared to dedicate his life in service to God, but it was the words that fell from the lips of a man who was to become his father-in-law that changed his destiny and gave him a place in the history books.

At a small church in Scotland, Andrew Moffatt, a missionary in Southern Africa, challenged the congregation to share his burden and God's love in a nation so vast and so dark where he, himself, had seen 'in the morning sun, the smoke of a thousand villages where no missionary had ever been.'

After hearing this, Livingstone gave himself to God and to Africa, and here, in a little village in Zimbabwe, was a living testimony to the lasting value of his life. In Livingstone's day, few people had ever gone to Africa, and those who did had incredible stories of paganism and cannibalism to recount. Now in many ways what was once the dark continent has become a continent of light, as nation after nation sees awakening to the gospel.

Zimbabwe was very unlike the Eastern bloc countries I had visited, but there again, there are many parallel needs. As socialism crumbles in Eastern Europe, so it has failed to live up to many of its promises in Africa. And while Zimbabwe is a socialist nation by name, it bears none of the characteristic trademarks that had blanketed Eastern Europe with socialist slogans and doctrine.

It was obvious on arrival at the village by the Livingstone Mission that these precious African people hadn't been affected very much by socialism or any other 'ism'. I wondered if anything had affected these people much.

As our car came to a halt in front of a small cluster of mud huts with thatched roofs, I wondered what I could contribute to these people who seemed so far removed from the world in which I lived. But very quickly it became apparent that something had indeed affected their lives.

The children came running to the car, barefoot and dressed in rags, yet squealing with delight.

'Khiwa!' ('White man!') they shouted to one another.

They were as fascinated with me as I was with them.

Samuel, our native friend, bellowed deeply, 'Come on everybody, let's praise God!' And suddenly, church began underneath a tree in the middle of the Zimbabwe bush land. About fifty people appeared and our service began.

African choruses were lifted up in full voice as more and more people came out from the bush. The people live in small family groups; a hut for Mum and Dad, one for the boys and another for the girls, and a smaller one for cooking. And a few hundred yards away, another family had a similar set up.

They were very gracious people who managed to find a couple of dining room chairs that they invited us to sit on. But I figured if they can praise God under a tree, I could certainly stand up while they did it. They are in no hurry in Africa. No one's looking at their watches—partly because they don't have any—but more than that, they are not so concerned with time as we are in the West. Because for them the most important thing is what you are doing at the moment, not what you have to do later.

And if you don't get to what you are supposed to do, you can do it another day. It's quite a change from a world where hamburger chains compete to deliver the fastest burgers in town to the desperately driven.

As we all continued to worship, the sky above us grew dark and then black, and warm drops of rain began to fall. I thought they'd probably wrap things up and we'd all go home, but it didn't seem to interrupt their singing. They offered us the shelter of one of their huts while they continued, but I realised that I was in danger of being more concerned about being wet than the real reason for my being there.

The rain came down harder and they asked me, 'Please share the word of God with us.'

All of my pre-prepared sermon thoughts seemed so insignificant at that moment. There was such an obvious difference in our lifestyles, and most of my ideas seemed more relevant to the culture in which I lived than this environment. These people didn't need to hear sermons on stress, success and the usual issues that face Western Christians! They still went down to the river to get water and lived without electricity and bathrooms. They were people who lived from day to day with no tangible income, no savings account, no nest eggs, just scratching a living out of the bush, selling firewood after a three-hour walk into the town to get enough money to buy food.

But we had a common denominator: our relationship with Jesus Christ. Not a Western Jesus, or for that matter an African Jesus, but a Jesus for everyman, regardless of his cultural lifestyle. And what these people wanted to hear was not a bunch of stuff about my life, but about him.

'Blessed are the poor in spirit, for theirs is the kingdom of Heaven,' was the Scripture that came to mind.

And as Samuel translated my words into the tribal tongue for the older people, I felt a strange kinship with these wonderful group of people sitting in the dirt as rain continued to fall.

Our service drew to a close as we sang yet another African chorus, and by the time we reached the comfort of our car, we were well and truly drenched. But as we drove off in our modern Japanese machinery, the congregation disappeared into the bush, cheerfully waving and shouting to each other as the rain continued to pour down. We were one of the few cars on the main road back into Bulawayo as we returned for our evening crusade in Luveve.

The worship died down in that evening meeting, and amid the unintelligible African dialect, I heard my name mentioned. Recognising my cue, I stood up once again to address the people.

A couple of days earlier, I had talked with a wealthy Indian man who had grown up in Zimbabwe. He was a Muslim. Our conversation had turned to his religion because I had seen a few Islamic butcher's shops and other references around town to that religion. I had asked him why the Muslim religion seemed to be growing. What he said had helped to reshape my thinking in a big way.

'The Christian missionaries came here many years ago. They did great work in this country and helped the people very much, not only spiritually, but physically as well, bringing education and medicine and generally helping the quality of life,' he said.

'They brought, of course, their gospel and told the wonderful story of Jesus and God's great love for what was then called Rhodesia. And they called the Africans to leave their tribal religions and follow Jesus Christ. The only problem was that many of them spoke of God's love and care for them, but then would not allow the African nationals to worship with them in their churches.

'Blacks and whites were separated and the work of the God of justice was undone by the foolish bigotry of man.'

Much has been nobly done in God's name, which in many ways has ultimately torn down rather than built up the work of God. And being in a country that had once known minority rule and repressive conditions for the nationals, I wanted to be careful not to build on that foundation, but on the true foundation of Jesus Christ.

In contrast to the Indian man's comments, I also saw the fruit of lives that had been given to God in sacrifice and poured out in love and service for the African people that stood out in spite of the overshadowing of some men's ignorance.

So as I spoke through my interpreter, Peter, I spoke about what I knew, not past policies or history, but about the love of God, so great that he gave his only son for a young man entrenched in Western culture and lifestyle and for these people who lived a life in which I had nothing in common.

There is power in the gospel of Jesus Christ, power to change lives no matter what their condition. And as I shared what God had done for me, the obvious barrier of my Englishness and skin colour was brought down gently as God's love filled that place.

I invited the people to make a commitment to Jesus, and as I spoke they began to stand until over half the room was on its feet. Having been in the whole service and seen the fervor of their worship, I thought perhaps that they had misunderstood my invitation and I said to Peter under my breath, 'I'm talking about coming to God to repent for sin and become born again. Why are so many people standing?'

'Because they are heathens, who have been convicted of their sin and recognise their need for God,' he replied with disarming simplicity.

'Why were they worshipping so passionately?' I asked.

'Because they are polite and Africans like to sing, but from now on, when they sing these songs it will be as men and women changed,' he said, his face beaming with a huge smile.

As the people thronged forward, the Burning Sisters took the platform again and, to great cheers and rejoicing, once again God's children in Africa raised a passionate chorus of praise to their God.

God is doing a marvellous work in Africa. The Dark Continent is dark no more. Many studies in revival are now being conducted across the vast African continent, as nation after nation sees great harvest into the kingdom of God. It is truly God's sovereign hand that has brought about great things, but I can't help but think that once again it's the incredible men and women of God in that continent who have helped shape what's going on. Willingly and fervently they give themselves to God, despite their obvious lack of the things that we would consider necessary to live.

It was another series of God's wonderful orchestrations that brought me to Africa. Samuel, a pastor and evangelist and our contact in the country, had come to the United States to visit a brother, who was studying at university in Texas, to try to gain support for his budding work in Zimbabwe. Around the same time I had been invited to appear on a Christian television programme to speak about rock and roll and Christianity.

Samuel was having a sleepless night, depressed because of continual rejection and a seeming inability to find anyone interested in his labour of love in Africa. In the middle of the night, he turned on the television and saw me during a re-run of the programme I had spoken on. They put my address on the screen and, for some reason—perhaps desperation— he felt that he should write to me.

I got lots of mail from my appearance on the television programme, some of it quite strange from various Christian faction groups that were either for or against what I had to say or who simply wanted me to listen to their particular doctrinal stance. But the thing that struck me from Samuel's letter was that he had come to America to find someone who'd reach out their hands and help the body. This, of course, was a role that I personally felt was appropriate to me—and, to a degree, to the well-equipped and affluent Western church. So we joined hands and began to labour together.

Once again, as I tasted of yet another country in this vast world, I was in awe of the incredible God that we serve, who takes our lives and makes such adventures out of them when we choose to live for him. The sight of all those people, tearfully coming to give their lives to Christ, will be permanently etched into my memory.

I used to hear a lot of people advocate the lasting value of rock and roll. And I've seen many people caught up in the moment filled with happiness, but their lives weren't changed, just touched for a moment, perhaps by a favourite song or a close-up look at their music idol.

But around the globe a revolution is taking place. People aren't just being touched, they are being changed. This revolution began not on the world's centre stage, but largely ignored. Not an event covered by the media, but heralded by few. This revolution wasn't staged by men of great power or influence, but began in seemingly innocuous circumstances in a small town in Israel.

But from those humble beginnings, the greatest revolution the world has seen was birthed. It is a revolution in the hearts of men of global impact. One that has continued for 2,000 years and is increasing as men and women from every tribe and nation on the earth come under the banner of God's love.

But still there is the smoke of thousands of villages, not only in Africa but around the globe, where no Christian has been to tell of God's love.

Shortly after I returned from Africa, I was given a most unusual Christmas gift. In a small red bag was a chunk of concrete about two inches long. It came along with a certificate of authentication that this was, in fact, a genuine piece of the Berlin Wall. What was once a symbol of isolation, repression and totalitarianism, came tumbling down while I was in Africa. Seemingly overnight the world had gone through tremendous upheaval, as nation after nation in Eastern Europe took to the streets with the cry of freedom on their lips.

We were all thrilled with the sight of thousands of Germans from East and West Germany being tearfully reunited after years of separation. Also the people attacking the Wall and pulling it down, not only in Germany, but in Czechoslovakia, Poland, Hungary, Bulgaria and, most dramatically, Romania, where men and women gathered en masse, protesting for change and an end to their repressive lifestyle.

We were therefore all the more stunned by the incredible response of the Chinese government to the student demonstrations in Tiananmen Square. This was a salutary reminder that not everybody is hungry for change, and that we live in a world where brutality and injustice have not been eradicated.

The twentieth century has been remarkable in the changes it has brought to the world. So much has happened in the last eighty to ninety years, but 1989 must go down as one of the most important years in history. It is to this world that you and I must present the gospel. Not an ideal of men that will bring temporary change, but a revolution from God that changes people for ever, a revolution that knows no barrier. I believe that the toppling of the Berlin Wall and the changes in Eastern Europe and many other countries around the globe are challenges to the church.

So what can you and I do? It would seem that nothing would make an impression, but outside of Bulawayo, Zimbabwe, in the middle of the African bush, is a little wooden sign that simply announces,

'David Livingstone Mission,' that proves if you give yourself to something lasting, you *can* make a difference.

Chapter Twelve

FOR SUCH A TIME AS THIS

God must have a great sense of humour, especially in the way he has guided my life in recent years. As I grew up as a boy in England, I thought about being so many different things. I day-dreamed about being the Milky Bar Kid, a train driver, then a dustman, later delivering early morning pints as a milkman and, finally, as being Superman. It was the general stuff that boys consider to be great career moves. However, I never once considered the possibility of a life in the church, which hardly seemed a career holding forth the promise of adventure and excitement.

But here I was in America, taking an active part in the church. It may seem strange, but I now find it hard to imagine doing anything else with my life.

After the transition of our move to the mountain paradise community of Lake Arrowhead, California, Cathy and I began attending a church where we could continue our life with God. It was a little wooden country church in the town of Rim Forest, the first you hit after navigating the narrow road up the mountain side. It was as much a shock for the congregation as it was for me. This was a small, tight-knit community in Southern California, containing Americans resplendent in their plaid shirts and cowboy hats.

Fortunately, they were very tolerant of a strangely attired Englishman who insisted on wearing leather trousers and earrings. I think the English accent once again came to the rescue. Cathy and I were embraced in true Christian love and grew close to the members of that fellowship.

Everyone liked it when I read the Bible in public. They thought I was reading it in purest King James English. That progressed into an invitation from the pastor, Jim Cobrae and his wife Deby, to share my unusual testimony with the church. From there they encouraged me and helped me develop and then gave an opportunity to teach home Bible studies. As time passed, I became the assistant pastor and eventually, when God called Jim and Deby to move, the post was offered to me.

It was the last thing that I ever imagined doing, but yet when the opportunity did arise, something inside me told me that this was the next step.

The thought of assuming responsibility for the spiritual wellbeing of God's people was, and still is, an awesome responsibility, and I assumed the task with a great deal of prayer and trepidation. But God is gracious; he doesn't call us to serve him because we're so great, but if we'll surrender our lives to him, he'll come alongside and help us in our weakness.

One of the primary concepts God has laid upon my heart is that he wants to use ordinary people. It's easy to forget the things that happen to us—life goes on and they become just memories. It's very easy in the world in which we live to allow those experiences to become fond memories, moments of excitement in our lives, and then to just carry on moving along in our world.

But I believe now that nothing I have experienced has happened by chance. I look back and see how God was working in me even when I didn't acknowledge his existence. And I truly believe it was the hand of God that allowed me to experience those times. I believe God's purpose in all this was to show me the futility of living a self-centred life. He called me, as a Christian, to live a life built on the worship of God and the serving of others.

I am convinced that God allowed me to go behind the Iron Curtain to call me to account for the life I was living. Not only is it easy to forget, but also to take the time we've been given on earth for granted. We become so consumed in our day-to-day existence that we have a tendency to live at a low level, pulled along blindly by our culture and environment, flowing along with the tide of humanity.

As Christians, God has called us to swim against the tide, to look at life from a higher perspective, to see our lives have purpose, and that we were put on this planet to live for God and bring glory to his name. That's why I have to take all my experiences and put them in the right perspective. In the Bible Paul wrote to Timothy, a young man who was facing the challenge of living as a Christian in a world very different and yet very similar to the one in which you and I live today. In order to do that, Paul exhorted him to live with passion, to recognise that God had called him; he told him to 'take heed to himself' (1 Timothy 4:16). He wanted Timothy to take stock, to pay attention to what he was doing with his life, something I had seldom done.

Going to Russia was, for me, a couple of weeks out of my life, a novel experience, but for the believers I came in contact with, it was reality. They had to live out their lives in that hostile environment. God allowed me the privilege of experiencing that so that perhaps I could 'take heed' for my own life.

Part of being a Christian means becoming involved in the world in which we live. It's very easy to develop an ivory tower theology and remove oneself from life and all of its difficulties, becoming harsh and judgemental, finger-pointing hypocrites who rant and rave about the many perils in the world. But God has left us on the earth to shine for him, to reflect his love, compassion and care for people.

One of the stories in the Bible that really touched my heart, and was instrumental in my taking steps in the area of mission, was that of Esther. It is contained in an interesting little book of the same name, in the Old Testament, and it's about a girl who won a beauty contest. God gave Esther beauty and that gift caused her to wind up as the wife of the King.

But beyond that God, who sees the beginning from the end, had a greater plan. As usual, the Israelites were having a tough time, and once more an enemy rose up and devised a plan to wipe them off the planet. Esther was locked up in the palace, far removed from her Jewish relatives, ignorant of what was taking place, but she had an uncle who was not prepared to give up without a fight and, even though the situation seemed impossible, he took action. His name was Mordecai. He tried to get her attention by covering himself in dust and sitting outside the Palace, screaming his lungs out. Not a good move in those days when the King didn't want to be bothered with anything that could be upsetting to him.

Esther first sent her uncle some new clothes to replace the ones that he'd ripped off in his anguish. He responded by sending back a message saying that he didn't want her clothes, he wanted her, her action, her involvement. She had a position of influence in the land and Uncle Mordecai wanted her to use it now.

He told her that she needed to go to the King and make a plea on behalf of the Israelites. Not too difficult a task—but there was just one problem: she couldn't go and visit the King unless he called her, and he hadn't done this in a long time. To go in uninvited meant almost certain death. Perhaps knowing the situation she was walking into, Uncle Mordecai told her it was silly to think that just because she lived in the palace, she would escape the disaster that loomed over the Israelites. So he ended his conversation with her with these words: 'Who knows whether for such a time as this you have come into the kingdom.'

That was Esther's problem, what to do with her life. It was all very well being a royal personage, living in luxury, but perhaps God had a greater plan. We can all relate to Esther. It doesn't matter what life we live, I believe there is a greater and higher purpose for us all, regardless of our occupation, financial status, or any fame or fortune we may have achieved.

Time was short. The commencement of the massacre of the Jews was close. Esther had to act, to decide how she was going to live. She replied to her uncle with what I regard as some of the most inspiring words in the Bible, 'And so I will go onto the King, which is against the law, and if I perish, I perish!'

For you and I, the scenario is very much the same. Daily we are faced with the choice of how we're going to live. Perhaps God's word to us is the same as

Mordecai's to Esther: we have come to the kingdom for such a time as this.

It is you and I who inhabit this world. Only we can affect it for God. Like Esther we've been gifted, perhaps not with beauty, but definitely with freedom. We're free to live the life of our choosing, but generally we choose to live lower than we should. We have closed eyes and closed minds to the world around us, too often content to let it all just pass us by.

But if God went to all the effort of Calvary to bring us into a relationship with him, and commissioned us to dwell on the earth as his representatives, perhaps we're taking too much for granted by living life on our own terms rather than his.

The world has been reduced to fit nicely in fifteen-second capsules into a 19″ colour television, so we can sit in the comfort of our living rooms and see the devastation that is going on—the upheaval in the socialist nations, the brutal repression in China where people desire freedom, a commodity they know little of yet are willing to give their lives for.

Our Christianity *can* be reduced into nice little rituals, catered to fit around our lives. We can tack Jesus Christ onto the end of our lives and not take action, and be lulled into thinking that we are living the life that God has for us.

But when Jesus Christ invaded my life, and permeated every part of it and exposed it for the folly that it was, he didn't just leave me with a consciousness of my stupidity; he cleansed me and asked me to follow him, to join that long line of human beings who, generation after generation, have chosen to swim against the current of popular lifestyle and make their lives count for God.

Jesus Christ committed the future of his gospel into

the hands of twelve ordinary, seemingly unqualified men. The odds against them were enormous, and yet because they chose to live with a passion for God in their generation, they managed to reach to the very edges of their world with the gospel. It demanded a lot of them. They constantly had to do battle with the pull of the world—the pressure to conform, to go the way that everyone else was going. But something inside them pushed them forward. Their hearts burned with the reality of what Christ had done for them and what he had called them to do. He had pulled them out of their worlds and invited them to share in his.

You have read a lot about me in this book but, in closing, I want to talk about you, whoever you are! You obviously haven't lived my life, but you've lived one of your own, filled with boring bits and good bits, a lot like mine.

The issue is, not the life you've lived up to now, but how you'll live the rest of it. Who knows whether, for such a time as this, you have come into the kingdom.

EPILOGUE

*How you can help Christians
in communist and post-communist countries*

Today we truly live in strategic times, even though two-thirds of the nations of the world are hostile to the gospel of Jesus Christ. The spread of communism, Islam and other types of totalitarian regimes have caused that number to increase to an alarming rate. These so-called 'restricted nations' have endeavoured in the past to close their borders to the work of the traditional missionary, and strictly curtail the activities of the Christians within their grasp.

Yet the light of Jesus shines in the darkness of these countries. Believers there continue to worship God together and proclaim the gospel, despite threats of imprisonment and death.

But often our brothers and sisters feel isolated and forgotten by the believers in the free world. They wonder if we know or care about their plight.

Today, with the *glasnost* experiment taking place, Christians in the free world have the opportunity to reach through the various curtains and let these heroes of the faith know that we have not forgotten them.

That's why I have become involved with a new ministry called ASSIST (Aid to Special Saints in Strategic Times). This non-denominational Christian ministry is designed to be a life-link between Christians in restricted nations and those in the free world. This can best be accomplished through personal contact—real people meeting real needs. A sister church programme has been established to help achieve this goal. As members of the church in the free world interact with their counterparts in a restricted country, lasting relationships are formed and the body of Christ is strengthened.

Wouldn't it be exciting to have your church or fellowship become a vital link in global Christian unity?

As a SISTER CHURCH

You will be able to:

* pray intelligently for your sister church as you learn of its needs

* pray for members of the church as you get to know them

* send letters and perhaps Bibles and other materials to your sister church

* visit your sister church when possible

* share your spiritual needs with your sister church by prayer

* respond to the material needs of your sister church

* encourage your sister church through expressions of love and concern

You will be blessed by:

* the prayers of your sister church

* spiritual growth by seeing how faith and love grow under suffering and persecution

* increased missions awareness as you become involved

* the love and encouragement of your sister church

We read in 1 Corinthians 3:8–9, 'Now he who plants and he who waters are one, and each one will receive his own reward according to his labour, for we are all fellow workers.'

We need to be *fellow workers* with our brothers and sisters who live in the restricted countries.

ASSIST'S ROLE

To serve you by:

* providing to both sister churches information about each other

* co-ordinating all travel arrangements

* making available Bibles, pastoral libraries and other literature to be taken to your sister church

* providing the training necessary for travel into restricted countries

* conducting ongoing research in restricted countries to profile underground churches and changes in their current situation

If you would like an application form to 'twin' with a church in a restricted country, or further information, please write to:

ASSIST Australia
P.O. Box A270
Sydney South
AUSTRALIA

ASSIST Canada
P.O. Box 483
Woodstock
Ontario N45 7YS
CANADA

ASSIST Europe
P.O. Box 789
Sutton Coldfield
Sutton Coldfield B72 1NB
ENGLAND

ASSIST
P.O. Box 41179
Pasadena
CA 91114-8179
UNITED STATES OF AMERICA

Streetwise

by John Goodfellow

John was hard. Tough on the streets, rough at home. Girls were like drugs—there for kicks; while alcohol seemed to keep life going.

Before long, John had found a real skill for fraud—yet deep inside he had a passion for truth. Was it to be found in the oriental religions, or the occult teachings of some of his friends.

If truth wouldn't come looking for him, he would travel the world until he found it. That's when life started to change, eventually leading him back to the people he had wronged, back to his family, and back to the streets that he understood so well.

Only this time he was more concerned with giving than taking.

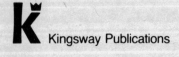

Kingsway Publications

Hungry for Heaven

by Steve Turner

Ever since Elvis Presley turned his back on a gospel career and Jerry Lee Lewis announced that he was dragging his audience to hell with songs like 'Great Balls of Fire', rock'n'roll has had religion on its mind. Some people, like Sam Cooke and Marvin Gaye, never resolved the pull between their earthly desires and their heavenly calling. Others, like Bob Dylan and Little Richard, sold out to God and upset their audience.

Almost all of rock'n'roll's innovators have experienced run-ins with religion. The Beatles championed Maharishi Mahesh Yogi, Pete Townshend became a follower of Meher Baba, Bob Marley was a devoted Rastafarian, The Rolling Stones investigated magic and Van Morrison's music is coloured by his individual brand of mysticism.

In this unusual and entertaining book Steve Turner chronicles the relationship between rock'n'roll and religion from Elvis to U2. He argues that the best rock'n'roll is truly a search for redemption, a search that can only be satisfied with a religious answer. He draws on extensive research and his own interviews with artists such as Jerry Lee Lewis, Ray Charles, Al Green, John Lennon, Mick Jagger, Pete Townshend, Van Morrison, Sting and Bono.

K

Kingsway Publications

Escape from the Storm

by Ivan Gorelkin

Why should God take one family and perform a series of miracles just so that they could escape to the freedom of the West?

Ivan Gorelkin's story is perhaps one of the strongest living parables of God's mercy today. Through answered prayer, dramatic visions and events that defy any natural explanation, a handful of Soviet citizens were lifted out of their home country and led to a land free from persecution.

There are many more that remain behind. Ivan knows that. Yet his story is a powerful reminder that God answers prayer and ultimately he is committed to the deliverance of all his people from evil and oppression.

Kingsway Publications